A TWIST OF THE WRIST

A TWIST OF THE WRIST

THE MOTORCYCLE ROAD RACERS HANDBOOK

by Keith Code

First Edition

ACROBAT BOOKS

Acknowledgements

Editorial Assistance
Bill Stermer
Michael Church

Help and Encouragement
Cort Sutton
Kawasaki Motors Corp., U.S.A.
Motorcyclist Magazine
Cycle World Magazine
California Superbike School

Design and Illustration
Cameron Ashby Associates, Inc.
Jeff Skrimstad

Important Lessons and Friends
Bob West
Mel Dinesen
Pierre Des Roches
Richard Davis
Griffith Park
L. Ron Hubbard
Judy Code

Photography
Kevin Ashby, page 80
Patrick Behar, pages 3, 74, 75, 79, 94, 95
Rich Chenet, page 82
Mush Emmons, page 17
Freud, page 42
Mary Grothe, back cover action photograph
Masako Takahashi, back cover portrait
Motorcyclist Magazine, page 14
Tom Riles, pages 26, 51, 56, 88
John Ulrich, page 109

California Superbike School, Inc.
P.O. Box 3107
Hollywood, California 90078

Copyright 1983 Keith Code

ISBN: 0-918226-08-2

Library of Congress
Catalog Card Number
82-73771

All rights reserved. No part of this book may be reproduced in any form or by any means without permission in writing from the author.

Printed in the United States of America

Warning: The riding techniques contained in this book are intended for racing purposes only. The author and publisher accept no responsibility for any accidents resulting in bodily harm or property damage that might occur from the increased speeds and rider ability that may be gained by the use of this material. The author and publisher do not guarantee that readers will attain the same high degree of riding skills that others have by applying these techniques. Supplemental notes and endorsements by noted riders that have used these techniques should not be taken as any guarantee as to safety or competency that might be gained, but merely as personal experience. If expert assistance is required, the services of a state licensed agency should be sought.

Always wear proper protective clothing and observe local speed laws.

Foreword

Even though I've only been road racing for two out of the twelve years of my career, it seems as though I've been doing it all along. Everything goes so smoothly now. If there's a problem, I handle it right away. Things are going right—they must be. I find myself in the winner's circle at almost every race. Of course my dirt track racing helped, but believe me, it wasn't always this easy.

My first time on the asphalt—for more than a couple of laps—was at the California Superbike School. It was really a good experience. I wasn't the fastest guy out there but it gave me the idea of what to do and, more importantly, that I did want to do it. Kawasaki had been helping me with my short track program. There are some great people down there who believed I had some promise, so they gave me a box stock racer and hired Keith Code to work with me for one year.

Here is the part that really surprised me: We spent days going over stuff that Keith had written down about racing. I thought we were going straight to the track, but here I was actually looking up words in the dictionary and talking about riding. After we did get to the track the whole thing turned around and there I was, writing down everything that I was doing on the track. Keith made me think *before* we got to the track, *while* I was on the track, and *after* I got off the bike.

I don't know if everyone can get into the winner's circle as fast as I did, but I know now that being able to think about your riding is important. Get that part done first.

This is where I started. I hope it works for you.

Wayne Rainey

Contents

▷ Margin Notes and Comments
by Eddie Lawson

Special Note:
Extra wide margins are provided for your notes.

THE VIDEO

See it! Fantastic cornering and braking. If you can see it, you can do it yourself.
Right?
Right! How hot a rider would you be if your tires never slid, you always had the right *reference points, brake markers* and turn points? You would be great!
Visualization is the key in all sports.

Being able to see it done brings life and excitement to ideas.
The "Twist Video" not only puts you in the rider's seat, but also shows *the right* and *wrong ways* to ride—and the results of both.
Cornering and braking are examined from above, beside and on the bike. You can see it.

Race tire technology is now available to everyone. Street tires win big time races and the "Twist of the Wrist Video" puts you in the rider's seat with how to use the new sticky rubber, and much more.
With the "Twist Video" *riding technology* is now equal to *tire technology. Get your copy today!*

107 MINUTES

The TWIST VIDEO is **$39.95** (CA residents add $2.50 tax)

CALIFORNIA SUPERBIKE SCHOOL P.O. Box 3107
Hollywood, CA 90078   (213) 484-9323

Author's Note

The information contained in this book is intended to be used by a rider to investigate and master the basic riding skills covered in each chapter. None of this information is magic. It has been developed during more than six years of training more than 2,500 riders and getting results that either improved lap times or increased rider confidence. This information works if it is applied.

There is a certain magic, however, in using information that is understood, and the best way to do it is one step at a time. Go over the information and really understand it, then go out and apply it, bit by bit. Mastering each point will establish a certainty that you can do it.

The things that Keith goes over in his seminars and book are things I do all the time. You can learn the same things.

Introduction

I'm going to begin this book with a little confession. I've never really been all that interested in racing–I just wanted to ride. Throughout my racing career I regarded the other riders on the track as mostly just a nuisance. Many times they got in the way of the observations I was making about my riding, about how I could improve my riding and how that information could be presented to my students. I've always had just as much fun riding along by myself in a race as I have competing with other riders.

My reasoning for this is simple–no matter how many other riders are on the track, you must still rely on your own ability. The track is the ever-present challenge–not the other riders. This idea has been strengthened over the years through my observation that the most successful racers can go nearly as fast in practice as they do in the race. They use their understanding on the track when they please, without the pressure of competition forcing them to "go fast."

Play the Game Well

Riding fast on a motorcycle is a tremendously exhilarating and challenging game. This game has rules and barriers. There's something to win, something to lose, and a purpose for each individual who plays the game. It demands your attention. The consequences of a major mistake can be severe–severe enough to make the game worth playing well. The purpose of this book is to describe the technology and the rules of riding fast so that every ride is a "win," so that you'll approach the barriers with confidence and understanding, and so you can further your purpose in riding or racing, whatever it may be.

My overall approach to rider improvement is: **To simplify the actions of riding by defining the basics, and by investigating the decisions you must make to ride well.**

What'll It Cost?

If your face shield leaks air, tape it up. The air won't come through and get your attention.

Attention, and where you spend it while riding a motorcycle, is a key element in how well you will function: **Attention has its limits.** Each person has a certain amount of it, which varies from individual to individual. You have a fixed amount of attention just as you have a fixed amount of money. Let's say you have a ten-dollar bill's worth of attention. If you spend five dollars of it on one aspect of riding, you have only five dollars left for all the other aspects. Spend nine and you have only one dollar left, and so on.

When you first began to ride you probably spent nine dollars of your attention on how to let out the clutch without stalling. Now that you've ridden for years and thousands of miles, you probably spend only a nickle or dime on it. Riders tell me that some common movements, like shifting, have become "automatic." It's not true. They are simply spending less attention on it. Riding is like that. The more operations you reduce to the cost of a nickel or dime, the more of your ten-dollars worth of attention is left for the important operations of riding or racing.

You must make hundreds of decisions while riding just one lap of a racetrack or one stretch of road—especially when riding fast. Hundreds! If you understand enough about riding to have correctly decided how to handle 25 of those situations, you are probably a fair rider. **The things that you do not understand are the things that will take up most of your attention.** Whenever a situation arises that you do not understand, your attention will become fixed upon it. You often fear a situation when you cannot predict its outcome, and panic costs $9.99—you may even become overdrawn. The course of action you have already decided upon to handle a potential panic situation costs much less than this and leaves you plenty of attention to sort out your options.

On the positive side, sorting out the actions of riding beforehand buys you the time and freedom to become creative with the activity of riding, just as having lots of change in your pocket allows you a certain freedom of movement. On the race track, that left-over attention allows you to experiment and to improve your riding ability.

High-performance riding and racing demand not only that you be able to perform the necessary actions, but also that you be able to observe them. Making accurate observations of your performance is the key to being able to improve them. **If you know what you have done— you know what can be changed.** If you did not observe what you were doing, the changes become haphazard and inaccurate. *Do you agree?*

In the next chapters we'll look at the game and where the attention is being focused or spent. We'll investigate the barriers to riding well and put into action the steps you'll take to bring home a "win" every time.

And finally, let's not lose sight of the basic reason we started riding—it's fun and makes us feel good. Here's readily available freedom, and all it takes is **A Twist of the Wrist.**

I might only use one-tenth of a cent on some things that cost another rider $5.00, but you spend something on everything you do on a race track. The better you get the less most things cost.

What Is a Rider?

Before launching into anything heavy, let's agree that the rider is the person controlling the motorcycle, not a passenger. The rider works the brakes and clutch, the throttle and steering. He determines whether the bike goes around the turn fast or slow, smooth or rough, up or down, and is the only individual who decides what action to take, carries it out, then decides how well it all worked.

It almost sounds too simple, but it's true: **What you do is what happens; what you don't do—doesn't happen.** Motorcycles don't do anything by themselves. They don't win races or lose them; they don't make mistakes or do anything right. Everything that happens during a ride depends solely on the rider.

Have you ever seen a new rider on the track or road struggling to operate his machine? The basic control operation, the track and who he is in relation to these are a mystery to him. He honestly feels he is being taken for a ride. If you've had those feelings, fine; even expert riders have felt this way at times.

There's an actual technology to riding. People are not born as good or bad riders—riding skill is learned. **A rider is a person who can lap a race track or ride down the road, fast or slow, and know what he did and how to change it.**

A TWIST OF THE WRIST

The Road You Ride

The Mysteries of Asphalt Revealed

Riders invariably have their favorite sections of road, the parts that flow together into a dance where everything happens just the way it's supposed to with no surprises. On the street or track, you know which ones they are—but you want to know why they're so comfortable. How much should you know about the road you ride? Which aspects are important and which are not? Why are some sections of road harder to ride than others?

First, some background. Highways are constructed so that motorists can travel from Point A to Point B very easily. The highway engineers are very thoughtful; they want to see you make it in one piece. The turns are often gently banked. Decreasing-radius corners are rare. Seldom is there a hairpin at the end of a straight stretch of road. Off-camber turns are avoided whenever possible. Corners are constructed in a predictable and straight-forward manner.

Designed to Fool You

A racetrack is another sort of beast. Not much of anything is done for your convenience. The designers have purposely constructed a course that will continue to create changing situations for the rider, to fool and challenge him. Hairpins are put into the most difficult sections, usually after the fastest straight, and "S" turns, or chicanes, often have a slower exit than entry. Corners may baffle you with several camber and radius changes to break your flow and force you into unusual situations. And always, the faster the turns are negotiated, the more difficult they become. There are, however, only five major changes that can be designed into an asphalt road. *Have you noticed this?*

Types of Road

1. Changes in Camber: A piece of road can have a positive camber—banking, or it can have "off," or negative camber. This means the

inside of the road is higher than the outside. Or, the road can be flat. A turn may be designed with any combination of these cambers.

2. Changes in Radius: A single turn may be a constant radius, as in a perfect half circle. It may decrease in radius, tightening up toward the end, or it may have an increasing radius, opening up at the end. Or it may be a combination of all three.

3. Series of Turns: In a series of interdependent turns, the line you take through the initial part of the turn will be partly determined by where you want to exit it to set up for the next turn. A series of turns can have any or all of the camber and radius changes listed above.

4. Uphill, Downhill and Crested Track Changes: Elevation can be added at any point to any type of turn or change in a road or track.

5. Straight Sections: These are sections where little or no turning is required. **Increases or decreases in elevation may be added.**

These are the five major changes that can be engineered into a piece of asphalt. With the addition of bumpy sections, which were not planned by the designers, you have all the possible situations. In order to understand a road or track, you must understand its characteristics. Each of these changes has a direct influence on you and your bike's progress through the corner. In order to ride quickly and safely, you must understand how these changes affect you and how you can best handle them.

Banked turns are comfortable for most riders. Understanding them allows you to take the full advantages they offer.

Positive Camber or Banking

Most everyone is comfortable riding a section of road that has some banking or positive camber. The banking has the effect of holding you up by creating a "wall" to push against with your tires. The bank also slows your bike down even more when you enter the turn because of the increased resistance created by this wall. Gravity is working for you, pulling you and the machine down the wall, counteracting the outward-bound cornering forces. *Some examples?*

It is very difficult to see the banking while you're riding on it. You may not notice a slight bank at all, unless you looked at the turn before you rode it. On the high banks at Daytona, after riding several laps on the outside tri-oval in a record attempt, the banked sections actually appeared flat to me and the pit area looked tilted at a 20-degree angle. It is easy to be deceived by even a small amount of banking because you're leaned over and don't have a straight view of the road. Also, the banking becomes less noticeable as you increase your speed.

Always design your approach so you can use the banking to your best advantage. Go low in the bank, close to the inside of the track, at the point where the banking begins to flatten out. This gives you and your bike the maximum holding advantage the banking has to offer before your bike begins to swing outward on the flatter section from the forces generated by acceleration.

In a turn, your bike and you are just like the weight you swing around your head on a rubber band. The faster you swing it, the heavier the weight becomes from centrifugal force, and the more it tries to swing to the outside. The banking "holds" you in until you move onto the flatter section of road that follows.

You can go into banked turns faster than it seems you can when you size up the turn and look at it from past experience. The banking will fool you initially and you will probably go into it much too slowly.

Also, when you are exiting a banked section of road to a flatter surface, you must straighten the bike since it will drag more easily when the banking is gone. Example: If you are in a banked section and are leaned over to the pegs, you must lean the bike over even more in relation to the track surface to keep that degree of turning radius when the bank is gone. If the bank is 10 degrees, you must lean the bike over at least ten more degrees to keep that turning radius on the flatter road surface.

The banking gives you more ground clearance than does a flat section of track. I have known riders who could run lap times on racetracks that were very close to record times and who had raced that same course 30 or 40 times, who finally discovered that one section of track was banked—that was why they could go so fast in that part. After knowing, they went even quicker. If you don't discover track angles, you might be getting away with riding maneuvers you feel you shouldn't be without even knowing why. Once you discover the reasons behind your abilities, you can begin to use the track to your advantage. *Will this improve your riding?*

Off-Camber or Negative-Camber Turns

I don't know any riders who regard off-camber turns as their favorites. These turns leave less room for error and definitely do not inspire confidence.

A turn that begins with a bank and ends off-camber demands the most changes and adjustments in lean angles. In order to continue around it, the bike must be leaned over farther. The effect is much the same as going from a banked to a flat surface. Gravity is now working against you, pulling you and your bike to the outside. You lose ground clearance. Therefore, you set up off-camber turns so that you are in the off-camber situation as short a time as possible—just the opposite strategy

On banked track you don't enter low and come out high.

as for a banked turn. Use straight lines on the parts of the track that are off-camber because you don't want to be committed to your maximum lean angle going into an off-camber section. Ideally, you would only commit yourself to the maximum lean angle at the very end of the section.

An effective alternative is to set up so that your greatest leaning occurs in the middle of the off-camber section. It has been called "squaring off" a turn or "going slow in the slow parts." It refers to the type of turn handling that allows you to straighten out the negative camber as much as possible. Basically, you enter as vertically as possible, then make the major steering change and exit as straight as possible.

Riders tend to see the basic turn more clearly because it is more obvious than the camber change. This is one of the deceptive tricks of the racetrack designer. The rider is sucked into the turn because he is basing his riding tactics on what the turn looks like instead of taking into account the changes in camber that can so seriously affect him. He must realize that gravity is now pulling the bike in the opposite direction of his intended turn, and the tendency of the bike to go toward the outside in an off-camber turn is dramatic. *Will this help?*

As speed increases, centrifugal forces generated by the bike/rider combination widen the cornering arc. The line must change as the speed goes up.

Flat Turns

Turns with no negative or positive camber–flat turns–will not increase or decrease the lean angle necessary to negotiate them at a constant radius or constant speed. Turn Two at Daytona is a great example of a basically flat turn with no radius changes, and most fast riders prefer to ride it on the inside. In turns of this kind, the fastest way through is the straightest line—it's also the shortest distance around the turn. In a flat turn there is no attempt to fool the rider unless a radius change is put in for variation. These turns commit the rider to his maximum lean angle and maximum speed for the longest period of time. Since you're going to be riding around the inside at max speed and max lean sooner or later, you may as well get down to it at the beginning. Taking a wide entry into a flat turn only gives someone a chance to pass you.

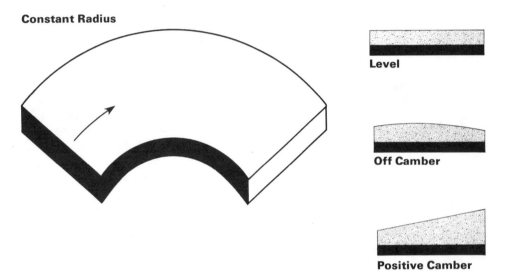

Constant Radius

Level

Off Camber

Positive Camber

Camber changes dramatically affect how a turn can be ridden.

Changes in Radius

Designers change the radius of a turn to put an additional twist in the action. Here are the basic kinds of radii and how to handle them on the track.

Constant-Radius Turn: A constant-radius (CR) turn neither increases (widens) nor decreases (tightens) as you go through it. As mentioned above, if it is a fairly long constant-radius (CR) turn with no camber changes, you will eventually wind up on the inside of the turn for most of it. If it is a short hairpin, you may have other options as to how to set up the entry and exit. In a really tight hairpin you must make an abrupt turning change—it should be done at the point at which you feel most confident. There is no rule as to how it should be done.

If a constant-radius turn has camber changes, it can act as a decreasing-radius (DR) or as an increasing-radius (IR) turn. For example, if the turn is banked on the entry and flattens out on the exit it will have exactly the same effect on your bike as the decreasing radius. If it is flat on the entry and banked on the exit, it acts as an increasing-radius. It is very common for amateurs—and professionals as well—to ride the turns the way they appear at speed and not the way they really are. It is very easy to have your attention stuck to the radius of a turn so you don't see the camber changes. Thus, knowing the location of the camber changes will help you greatly in a turn. *Where does this apply?*

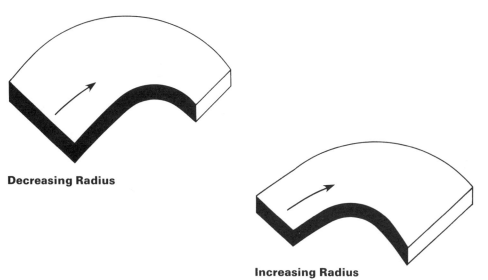

Decreasing Radius

Increasing Radius

The notorious decreasing radius turn. Designed to invite you in faster than it lets you out.

Usually easy to ride, the increasing radius turn can be made difficult with camber changes.

Decreasing-Radius Turns: This is a turn that tightens up as you go through it. In a decreasing-radius (DR) turn, the designer tries to trick you into treating it as a constant-radius, single-apex turn. If you fall for that, you must do one of three things: 1) Run wide at the exit, 2) Lean the bike over more at the end of the turn, or 3) Back off the gas so that one and two above don't happen.

A decreasing-radius turn has at least two apexes. Try to cheat the turn out of one apex and it will get you back with the other. In a DR turn you must ride what is there: don't try to make the turn into something it is not. Some misleading information has been circulating for years which says you "late apex" DR turns. This may be true in a very tight DR turn, but in a larger turn you must double-apex the turn.

You can make the turn longer for yourself by taking a wide entry line. This keeps your speed up and cuts down on the abruptness of the actual steering change. A DR turn that is flat on the entrance and banked at the exit will act as an IR or CR turn, depending upon the severity of the banking. If a turn is constructed so that it forces you to go slow at some point, you must decide where to go slow instead of letting the designer decide for you. By figuring a turn correctly, you ride the track—the track does not ride you. If you make a big mistake in line, you have probably just been sucked into riding the track the way it looks rather than the way it is.

Some places you have to use a real wide line so you don't scrub speed off, but not always.

Increasing-Radius (IR) Turns: This turn widens—its angle becomes less severe—as you go through it. An IR gives you the safest feeling because you have room at the end to make changes and corrections. You can easily recover from going into an IR turn too fast because you have plenty of room. An IR turn can be changed dramatically by the camber of the road, just as the DR turn can be. If it is banked going in, and flat or off-camber at the exit, it will act as a CR or DR turn, depending upon how much negative camber it has. **The radius of the turn is usually second in importance to its camber.** *Are you aware of this?*

Series of Turns: Two or more turns linked together in such a way as to influence each other are called a series of turns. They're usually designed to slow you down at a place where you otherwise could go faster.

For example: the entry into a two-turn "S" is faster than the exit. If the entry is taken as fast as possible, it will spoil the exit. If the entry is approached with the exit in mind, the rider will sacrifice some speed going in for a more constant drive out of the turn. Often this is a better strategy than having to back off and set up again for the exit.

It is very distracting to make this kind of change in the second turn in a series. Kenny Roberts has often said that you must go slow in some place in order to go fast in others—his "slow," of course, would put most of us into cardiac arrest. Here again, the designers attempt to lull us into taking action either too soon or too late. In some high-speed chicanes, being temperate with the throttle on the way in and setting up a smooth exit is worth over a second in lap time. Chicanes such as those at Pocono, Daytona and Sears Point are good examples. *Can you apply this?*

Uphill, Downhill and Crested Turns: When a track changes in elevation, it can create some exciting changes in how it must be ridden. Uphill and downhill sections of a track don't pose any particular problem unless they are in conjunction with a tricky camber change, radius change or both. Difficulties in up and down sections usually arise where there is a crest or sharp rise followed by a downhill. At this point the bike will feel light and will actually be light on the pavement. Braking over a crested hill is tricky because the downward pressure of the bike is lessened. This results in less traction.

A turn with a crest in the middle is also tricky because the bike tends to stand up and go toward the outside. Again, there is a loss of traction. It has the same affect as a short patch of off-camber road. It is best to go over a crested road as vertically as possible. *Any examples?*

On uphill sections where you must brake, you have the advantage that you can stop or slow the bike faster than on flat or downhill sections. If the hill that you're braking on has a 15-degree slope, the force of gravity pulling you back and down gives you a 27 per cent better stopping factor. You can use the brakes 27 per cent harder without locking them up, and that's a lot! On a downhill section the situation is reversed; the brakes lock more easily. The other possible problem with uphill, downhill and crested roads is that bikes tend to wheelie over them. This isn't really a problem unless you have to make a turn while the front wheel is still in the air.

Straight Sections: These are straight portions of track with no turns or changes to affect you. Straightaways are a great place to relax for a second or two. Check to see that you are breathing regularly. Riders often hold their breath during intense riding, which slows their efficiency. Lack of oxygen is one cause of muscle cramps while riding.

The road you ride, whether it be public or racetrack, is made up of the five components: camber, radius, elevation, series of turns and straights. How these components are combined determines your approach to riding them, not only where speed is the consideration, but for safety's sake as well. The purpose of a racetrack is to test and retest your riding skill; it is intended by the designers to be difficult. Your task is to unravel the mysteries of the construction by using your knowledge to your advantage. No amount of bravery will substitute for understanding, and no amount of suspension changes will entirely overcome the forces generated by these five components. *Do you get it?*

Note: Track Surfaces

Most race tracks and canyon roads are constructed from asphalt compounds. Asphalt can be, and often is, mixed with various substances to create different types of road surfaces. Race tracks, for instance, often have ground-up sea shells or granite chips mixed into the asphalt to give tires a better surface to bite on, and therefore better traction. The compounding is often very different from track to track and road to road, which is one of the reasons tire choice has become a very critical element in racing.

Other factors, especially heat, play a huge role in determining what tire will be the best that day. An overcast day that does not allow the track surface to heat up may require a different tire than a sunny day, even if air temperature is the same. Asphalt surfaces that are darker in color heat up more than lighter-colored sections. This is the case at Sears Point Raceway in Sonoma, California, where the track is a composite of three or four different asphalt compounds. Tires that work very well in one area tend to slide around in others. And tires that work well in the morning, before the track has heated up, sometimes will not provide good traction in the afternoon—and vice versa.

The amount of rubber on the track also makes a difference in traction. I have heard it said that traction is better after an auto race where a lot of rubber has become imbedded in the asphalt; I've also heard riders say it was not as good. My own observation is that lap times are faster after the track has a good layer of rubber on it, especially from an automobile race—providing there aren't loose pieces of rubber on the track surface.

Tires and asphalt are an entire technology unto themselves and I will not try to deal with them in this writing. By the time you read this, the technology will already have changed and there will be new tire compounds—better than what we now have.

You've got to be able to "read" pavement. I can tell whether I want to push it or not. There are a lot of kinds of pavement. Sometimes the ones that look like they are really going to be sticky are just the opposite.

9

CHAPTER TWO

What You Do

You Become A Scientist

The rider's ultimate weapon is his ability to perform the actions of riding, and to **be able to observe and remember what he has done.** This is a key to improvement.

Don't Badmouth Yourself

Many riders have a bad habit of talking in negatives about their riding. "I didn't go in hard enough," "I should have gotten a better drive off the corner," "I don't use the brakes that well," "I need to get a better line through this turn." Didn't. Can't. Shouldn't have, Don't, Too much, Not enough. Most riders use these negative words much too often. How can information about what he didn't do right, or things that were almost—or not quite—done, ever improve his riding? If a person is riding at all he is already doing more right than wrong. The job is to add to those correct actions and drop the incorrect. *Do you do this?*

You Can't Correct What You Didn't Do

The only way to make changes in your riding is to change what was done. To do that you have to know exactly what <u>was</u> done, not what <u>wasn't</u>. You didn't do a lot of things on that last lap—you didn't wash your car, you didn't go to church, and you didn't do just about everything else there is to do in life. You only did what you did. Don't fall into the trap of trying to correct your riding by looking at what you didn't do. This leaves you nothing to change. "I don't brake late enough in Turn Two," sounds innocent enough, but what information does it contain for you to improve? If you say instead, "I started braking at the asphalt patch just before the number three marker, and now I know I can brake even later than that," you know what was done and now have something to change.

It's simple—think of your riding in negatives and you don't have anything to change. Look at it the way it was and you <u>have</u> something to change. Negative thinking is incredibly non-productive. **Changing some-**

thing you didn't do is impossible. Thinking negatively about your riding puts you into a maze. A mirror maze works like that—it gives you nowhere to start your thinking from, then disorients you by covering up where you've been and where you can go. You have no reckoning point. The maze tries to make you lose a firm point of direction by opening up many possibilities. When you have a firm idea of where you came from you can always go back to that point and start over. It's the same on a race track. If you know just what you did, you have a stable base from which to make corrections on the next lap. *Will it work for you?*

Riding is One Thing—Riding Plus Being Aware of What You Are Doing is Quite Another

You have only so much attention to spend on what you are doing, your ten-dollar bill. If you spend it all on just riding and none on observing what you're doing, you can go quite fast. But if you spend five dollars on riding and five on observing yourself and what you're doing, you have something to look at and change when you return to the pits. You don't have to hope you can work yourself into a fever pitch to go faster—you can go faster by figuring out how to do it better.

How do you develop this wonderful ability to ride and observe what you're doing at the same time? You simply decide to <u>do</u> it. **You make an effort to look at what you are doing <u>while</u> you are doing it. Try it.** If you already have a record of your lap times on the track, go out and make an effort to observe yourself. The first thing you'll notice will be that you went slower while doing both the riding and observing. It costs a lot of attention to do both things at once. You won't be willing to ride as hard. Don't give up. You're spending a lot on looking and a little less on doing.

I know what I look like going through the turns. It might look ugly, but it works.

I go slow in the first practice, look at the track and get the feel of the bike.

An accurate mental recording of what you do on the track is invaluable.

11

Take It as a Whole

Now, take an entire practice session on the track and try to observe everything you're doing. Come back to the pits and think it over. Then, take the next practice and just ride. You'll notice one of two things: 1) You went faster, or 2) the riding became less work than before. It's also possible that both things happened—you went faster with less effort.

Riding with less effort means that you're spending more of your attention on what's important and less on just being ready for surprises. If you don't know what's coming up in a turn, you will be tense. If you have taken some time to observe what was happening, you have spent less attention on possible surprises.

It Costs More Attention to Keep Something From Happening Than It Does to Make Something Happen

As in anything, when you first begin to observe what you're doing it will cost you a lot of attention. After you become more comfortable with it you will spend less attention on it. It may take a rider a year or more to decide it's okay to slide the rear tire a bit on certain parts of the track. He might pick up one to five seconds by doing it. But before coming to that decision, which may take only a split second on the track, he might have been spending almost all of his attention in trying to keep the rear wheel from spinning and slipping.

Observing where and what happened on the track will make something like a little rear wheel slide a predictable part of riding. A rider who observes a drop in lap times, and also notices where he was sliding and what brought it about, has something to base a decision upon—he can decide if the sliding was helpful or if it didn't work and should be stopped altogether. *Does it make sense?*

Observing Is the Basis for Change

When everything is right you can tell exactly which laps were good.

If you go out on the track and run a better lap time, but have not observed what you did to cause it, you will not be able to strengthen the actions that worked. Riders who just ride and don't observe believe that everything that happened on that lap must be reproduced exactly and in the same order for them to repeat a good performance. This is one of the ways riders become superstitious. **Because they don't know what helped, riders go about trying to keep all factors the same as they were at the time they rode well.** You <u>can</u> keep things the same, but only by observing what you did and by deciding which factors worked best. **Observing what you do is the key to learning by your mistakes.**

You can easily cheat yourself out of the knowledge to be gained from mistakes. Let's say you got into a turn a little too hard and went wide of your line. Normally, you would try to get back to that good line—to what worked. That's fine, but there's a twist. If you "ride out your mistake," you will learn how that different line works. Trying desperately to get back to the ideal once you've made a mistake won't tell you anything except that you've made a mistake. Riding out that mistake will give you valuable information about how to handle it should it ever happen again.

Everything you do may be a little wrong, but at least you'll know what happens—and that's the starting point for change. Riders have been known to adapt a completely new method of riding after making mistakes. **Ride a mistake out and see what happens.** It will cost you more attention to try to keep something from happening than to go through with what you have started. *Do you think it will work?*

By the Time You Notice a Mistake It Is Too Late To Correct It

You may have heard this before—it's true. Once a mistake occurs on any lap or in any turn, you can't roll back the clock or the asphalt to correct it. You'll just have to make the best of it. Figure out what went wrong and correct it on the next lap.

It Is the Last Thing You Did That Got You Into Trouble

The root of the mistake is the control change or decisions you made and acted upon just before the problem occurred.

A good example of this is going into a turn too wide. The rider got there because it was where he had pointed the bike the last time he had made a steering change. Most riders would say, "I didn't turn soon enough." That isn't true. Actually, he kept it pointing straight too long. It will take a lot longer for the rider to realize what happened if he begins looking for the problem from when he noticed it than if he goes back to the earlier point of where he was steering before he began the turn. **He has to realize that he was operating from an earlier decision to go straight, not the later one to turn.** *Does this apply to you?*

If You Decide Upon the Wrong Explanation for a Mistake, the Solutions for It Will Also Be Wrong

This is another basic reason for being a careful observer of **what you do.**

Being able to ride is important, but riding and observing leads to understanding.

CHAPTER THREE

The Product

Developing Precision with Understanding

What is the line through Turn Three? What is the best **line** through any corner? Why is one rider's line so different from another's?

50 Years of Improvement

Lines used to be easier to figure out. A lot of racing theory has been developed in the last 50 years of racing, and that's a lot of history to back up the ideas that still haunt us from the 1950s and earlier. On a motorcycle, it was reckoned, the straightest line through the turn was the fastest way, or "line." But things have changed today. It was true then, but it's not necessarily true today.

Physics and natural laws have not changed—tires and suspensions have. In the '50s and earlier, riders were limited by the lack of sophisticated technology. They had to take the smoothest, straightest, shortest line through the turns because the hard-rubber tire compounds and non-compliant suspensions of the early days made abrupt changes in direction, braking on rough or rippled surfaces, over-enthusiastic braking while leaned over and other current-day riding possibilities simply out of

State of the art? Good enough to win Laconia in 1965. . . .

the question. If you had owned a set of Dunlop Sport Elites in 1950 and had gone to the Isle of Man on a 1980s Kawasaki GPZ 550, you probably would have won the race. That's a <u>street</u> bike with <u>street</u> tires today.

Tire and suspension technology have made it possible to ride more than one line through a turn and make it work. Riding styles have changed very dramatically since the 1950s, but the outdated rider information from those days still confuses some of us in the '80s. A fresh look at rider information and technology can help you ride better now.

<u>Definition</u>: A product is something that is produced; it is the end result when all the work is done. A product is what you can hold in your hand—or in your mind. You can turn it over to see if it can be produced better or differently, corrected or left alone.

Product of the Turn

A turn or series of turns has a "product." It is that point where you can say, "I'm done with that turn now–here's what I did this time, here's what happened. Now, what can I do to improve it?"

The simplest way to recognize that spot is to remember where you were brave enough to think, "I could go through that one quicker." **When you have enough attention left to review your progress, and the turn is no longer affecting you, <u>that</u> is when you're done with it.** *Have you experienced this?*

At that point, the sum total of everything you did in the turn is neatly wrapped up; you know that what you did either worked or it didn't. Some parts of the product were assembled correctly–maybe some weren't. This product has a location on the track, which for example might be a point three feet from the outside edge or just next to "that patch" of asphalt. This point on the track now reminds you of exactly where you're finished with the turn for that lap.

Other Factors

Other factors, besides your location on the track, are important parts of the product: what gear you're in, your speed at that point, your body position on the bike. Usually some amount of lean angle. The amount of control you have over the bike. The steering action you are–or are not-taking. Throttle action. Tire traction. Your impressions of what you did and how well it worked out. And a comparison of this pass through the turn with your earlier passes. All of these, and more, are part of <u>your</u> product for that turn. **The quality of your product is determined by all of what happened and how it worked.** *Any thoughts on this?*

<u>Note</u>: You use that product to develop a set of <u>known</u> circumstances that can be thought over and changed when necessary. A sub-product is a definite set of <u>known</u> circumstances that lead to the product for that turn.

Both your **products** and **sub-products** have an exact location on the track. There is no universal **product** or **sub-product**–they will be slightly different for each bike and rider. **Your product is a known destination along a known route.** You are supposed to know where you're going on a track, and the **product** is the place you are going. The guy with the best **product** wins. The **product** and **sub-products** are the result of a pre-determined and pre-decided plan of action, based upon your knowledge of the parts of that turn, and your knowledge of how to get your machine around it.

End back to beginning.

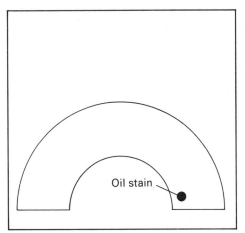

The Product is where you are done with the turn. It is a place you know.

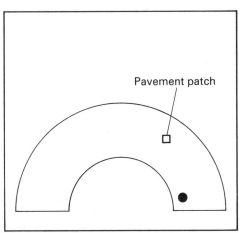

A Sub-Product alerts you that you are on the right track to your Product. You see it.

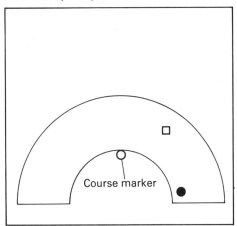

You locate another Sub-Product or Reference Point to guide you through the turn.

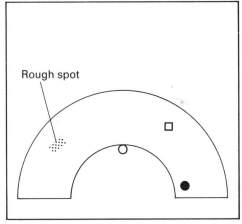

Each new RP leads to another that you know is going to be there.

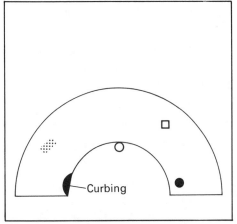

You build confidence by knowing where you are on the track with the RPs.

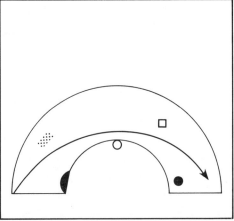

You become able to "see" the turn before you even begin to go through it.

David Emde performing miracles on 250cc GP bike. At 185 pounds and 6'3" tall, his "plan" is different than yours.

Your Line Is Your Plan

From talking to most riders, it is easy to believe that once you find the **"right line"** for a turn, everything will magically turn out OK and your lap times will improve because of this knowledge. It isn't true.

I once experimented with showing others the **"right line"** through the turns of a race track. I had students follow me lap after lap at moderate speeds as I did precisely the same thing at precisely the same place on the track each lap. The student was then asked to repeat the procedure that had been shown to him. I never found a student who could do it exactly. Eddie Lawson observed this same thing while instructing **California Superbike School** students at Loudon. Only one rider out of 25 was able to reproduce his line after being shown. (Actually two riders were able to do it. The other was my 12 year old son, who Eddie offered to sponsor afterwards.)

I've placed myself in the same situation and asked a better rider to show me his **"lines"** around the course. The course was Ontario Motor Speedway, 3.19 miles and 20 turns; the rider was then-250cc U.S. champion, David Emde, who was all but unbeatable that year on the ¼-liter machines. We went around the track at a good practice pace as I carefully observed what he was doing in hopes of finding out some deep, dark riding secrets.

I did find out. I found out that **a rider's line is his plan for going through a turn.** His plan is based upon what he does well and what he doesn't do well. I observed, then and now, that a rider's plan will be based upon his strengths and weaknesses. His line is the result of how his strengths and weaknesses fit together.

For example, riders who use the maximum amount of lean angle the bike has to offer will usually design their **"line"** to use lean angle to their advantage. Their **"line"** is often tight to the inside of the turn. By contrast, a rider who does not use all of the ground clearance available to him will design his **"line"** (plan) so that he does not have to spend so much time leaned over to the maximum. He will finish his steering as soon as possible, straighten the machine and move away from the turn as vertically as possible. All riders will design their turns around the strong points they believe they have.

When the Superbike School was at Loudon I let 24 riders follow me around the track so they could see my line. Then I followed them to find out how they were doing. Twenty-three of them got it wrong from what I could see.

The thing about riding on the back of a motorcycle with someone else driving is that they never do it exactly like I would and it scares me.

If someone pulls me I change my line in that turn and see if it works. I have films of me racing with riders and I'll pull them five bike lengths off a turn and still they just keep on doing the same thing. If the other guy's plan is better you can fit it into yours and beat him.

Learning a Line

Following another rider can be very instructional if you can determine his **plan** by watching him. If his **plan** is better designed to handle a turn than yours, and you can see **why** it is better, you may have learned how to use your own abilities to better handle some track situations. The value in following another rider–if there is any–is in understanding his plan and being able to expand your own riding because of it. It's not in learning the **line;** it is learning the **plan** that counts.

Basic Goal

Your basic goal in any turn is **getting through the turn with increased mph, decreased time spent in it and adequate control of the bike.** You are looking for **drive** out of the turn that will carry you to the next turn or down the straight in the shortest amount of time with the greatest amount of speed. Of course, you must still be in control of the bike. You balance the factors of speed and time to get the best **product.** Yet it is possible to come out of a turn faster than before and still not decrease your lap time. Turns can suck you into making mistakes like that.

Turn Balancing

Getting the best **product** from a turn requires **turn balancing:** this is where you balance your speed out of the turn against the amount of time it takes you to get through it. The most common mistake riders make is to go into the turns faster and faster, then come out of them at the same speed or slower. **It's easier to go into a turn faster than it is to come out faster. Going in too fast can cost you your drive coming out.** You've got to be able to carry a faster entrance speed through the exit of the turn to improve your lap times. Going in too fast, then fouling up in the middle of the turn, will lower your exit speed.

Turn balancing is like your ten dollars worth of attention. Figure that you have only so many miles per hour (MPH) to spend in a turn on any particular lap for any particular line. If you spend your MPH unwisely at the beginning of the turn, you don't have them at the end. Excess speed at the wrong time can cost you time. Don't jump at the first chance you get to go faster. The increased speed you have as you exit one turn will be added to the speed that you carry all the way to the next. Don't burn up MPH at the beginning of the turn; use **turn balancing** to produce your correct **product: Increased MPH, decreased time spent in the turn and the bike still under control at the turn exit.**

Find the Product

How do you find the **product?** Let's assume you have ridden the track for a few laps and have figured out what the designer has engineered into this piece of tarmac. You have studied the radius changes and the camber changes (see Chapter One, "The Road You Ride"). You're suspicious of the turns on a race track and know they're meant to challenge and fool you. With this information you have a good idea of how every turn affects you and your bike. You become aware of what the **product** is for **you** and your machine by applying that information and experience from riding. Now you have a starting point, a place on the track to work with, correct and change, to make decisions about.

Having a product in mind for a turn is like having a road map and a destination for a trip. You'd have a very hard time getting to your destination if you didn't know where it was. You can't get from New York to Kansas City unless you know where Kansas City is!

Obtaining a precise **product** for a turn is the first step in deciding how to improve that product. **Having no product is like having no destination.** *Do you agree?*

Having your end point (product) well known, even in wide open sweepers, creates confidence.

End to Beginning

You must work from the end back to the beginning of the turn to establish your **product.** Decide in advance, before you go into the turn, where you are going to exit. You must be able to "see" the **product** of the turn in your mind as you enter it. This enables you to keep the pieces and parts of the turn working toward that product. This **overview** allows you to figure out each step necessary to arrive at the product or destination.

You can become hopelessly lost by continuing to "look" at a turn from beginning to end instead of from the end back to the beginning.

Once you know where you're going, you can spend your attention more wisely on the problems that come up in the turn, such as tire slippage and passing. You'll have plenty of spare change left to handle them. Otherwise, without a **product** and destination, you will always be spending too much attention on what is going to happen at the end of the turn. Keeping your **product** in mind helps you handle the uncertainty.

I go out and set my plan and a lot of times the first one is the best. If it doesn't feel right I change it, maybe every lap.

Once you have a **product,** whether it is perfect or not, you can use it as a yardstick to measure your progress. Any changes you make in the turn will change the product somewhat. You will be able to tell whether those changes are working or not. As you increase your speed through a turn, the **product** will change slightly–or perhaps a great deal if you're a beginner. An experienced rider may make a change that is three feet back from his previous **product** and one MPH faster. A beginner's **product** may change 10 feet, and may be a gear higher and five MPH faster during the course of a day on the track. A **product** gives you something to shoot for–something to change. If you blow the turn, you can always go back to a less aggressive or slower **product** and get through it well enough.

Locate the Product

Where and how you enter a turn is totally decided by what and where the product is. Only rarely will you go into a turn the way it looks from the approach and have it work out well in the end. New and inexperienced riders commonly begin the turn too early because they have no **product** in mind. Even pros can be seen doing it. This opens the door to a lot of mistakes and uncertainty.

A product is made in stages, one step at a time. These stages of its development are marked by **sub-products. Sub-products** also have a location on the track and other factors that are similar to an overall **product.** Lean angle, speed, body position, amount of control, steering and more are the **sub-products** you can use as indicators to tell you how you're progressing toward your **product.**

Medium-speed and slower-speed turns will produce more **sub-products** than faster turns. You don't have the time to make a lot of changes in faster turns, and you must make them as simple as possible to leave yourself enough attention to do it right. Usually, fast turns do not have multiple camber or elevation changes–if they did they wouldn't be fast turns. Slow and medium-speed turns often have these kinds of changes, and they often require dramatic steering changes. For you to reach the desired **product,** these changes must be made at precise places on the track. These are **sub-products—places that require a change in order to reach your product for that turn.** Changes in gears, steering, throttle, braking, body position and the points where you look for course markers are all **sub-products.** *Any examples?*

Point of Entry

Just as the end **product** has a precise location on the track, so does the beginning point, the point of entry where the major steering change for the turn occurs. This is a **sub-product.** In banked turns, your entry point should always be designed to use the banking to best advantage coming out of the turn. What happens to you and the bike when the banking flattens is always a **sub-product,** a change. Precisely locate the point of your major steering change going into the turn so you can have something to adjust, a point to think from. The emphasis is to use the banking to your advantage. You can think of it as "connect-a-dot" riding.

If you "go into" turns too soon, you are committed to maximum speed and lean angle for a greater portion of the turn, which leaves you fewer options for corrections, and you feel you can't or shouldn't make any changes in your line. Now passing, grounding out on bumps, steering, throttle and gear changes all become matters of great concern and become more difficult to do smoothly. Going into turns too soon is your indicator that you do not have your **product** well defined, that you're slightly lost. **Not knowing where you're going in a turn invites you to go in too soon.** The track designer fools you into riding the turn the way it looks at the beginning rather than the way it will work out in the end. Working out the **product** and **sub-product** provides a map through the turn.

Faster Is Deeper

Here's another way of looking at it: if you make your major steering change at the same point going into a turn–and increase your speed past that point–you will run wide of the point you passed on the last lap because of the increase in centrifugal force. If the bike runs a bit too wide at the exit, you may believe you went too fast. Actually, the remedy is to go in deeper before making the steering change. **The faster you wish to go through a turn, the deeper you have to enter it to increase your speed at the exit.** *What will change if you do this?*

If you go in deeper and faster, the steering change will need to be more abrupt, and the bike will not want to turn as easily as before. The trick to going in deeper is to go a bit slower right at the point where you make your steering change. You must learn to restrain yourself. As Kenny Roberts says, "Learn to go slow to go fast." If you do it right, you'll be able to go faster from that point on through the turn. The bike can be straighter up and down, less committed to maximum lean angles and speed, so you can adjust your speed and set up a **product** more easily. The important part is knowing **where** you went into the turn so that you have something to change and adjust. This is a **sub-product,** and an important one.

Old Racer's Tale

Another important point is the false idea that you must use up all the track at the exit of a turn, whether you have to or not. Perhaps this comes from the old cornering theory that says you begin the turn wide and exit it as wide as possible. Wherever it comes from, it not only isn't always true, but it can actually prevent you from going faster through the turns.

How? **If you let the bike go wide at the exit, just because there is track left over, it can give you a false impression you're going as fast as you can.** You can fool yourself into believing it can't be done faster. As you're figuring the turns and dialing in the **product,** you use the information you've stored up from the last lap to decide if any changes can be made. **If your information says you went all the way to the edge of the track the last time through, it makes it difficult to decide to go faster this time.** You know the bike will go wider if you go faster, and you'll run out of track. Your **product** will change. You won't feel as confident that it can be done. *Will it work for you?*

Hold That Line

The remedy for this common error is to **hold the bike to the tightest line possible on the exit so you can get an accurate idea of where that speed takes you on the track.** Where the **product** of that speed puts you. If you hold your line down at the end of a turn and there is still eight feet of track left, you could safely assume you can go faster. If the next time you keep everything the same going into the turn, using the same line but increasing your speed, and you <u>still</u> have five feet of track left, you can go even faster yet. The point is, don't fool yourself by using up the track when it isn't necessary.

By handling the exits of most turns in this way, you can begin to establish a very accurate **product** and good **sub-products.** You're engineering the turn to fit your riding and equipment, deciding on a **product,** then making adjustments to improve upon it. You are not being taken in by the track, making useless changes just because there's an opportunity to do so.

A good example of being sucked in on the entrance of a turn is the old trap of the decreasing-radius turn. You go in fast because you can, then have to play some serious catch-up at the point it begins to tighten. Holding your speed down on the entrance can give you the exact information you need to go faster—if it's possible. That's you thinking now, not sucking yourself into making an error. *Where will you try it?*

Your Results

The **products** and **sub-products** give you a destination and accurately mark the places where you can make changes on the road. They are your way of breaking down the process into smaller parts you can understand and change. Your confidence and smoothness increase when you know where you're going and what to do when you get there. Your basic requirement as a rider is to observe where your **products** and **sub-products** are, what to do at those points and to remember them so you can make use of them.

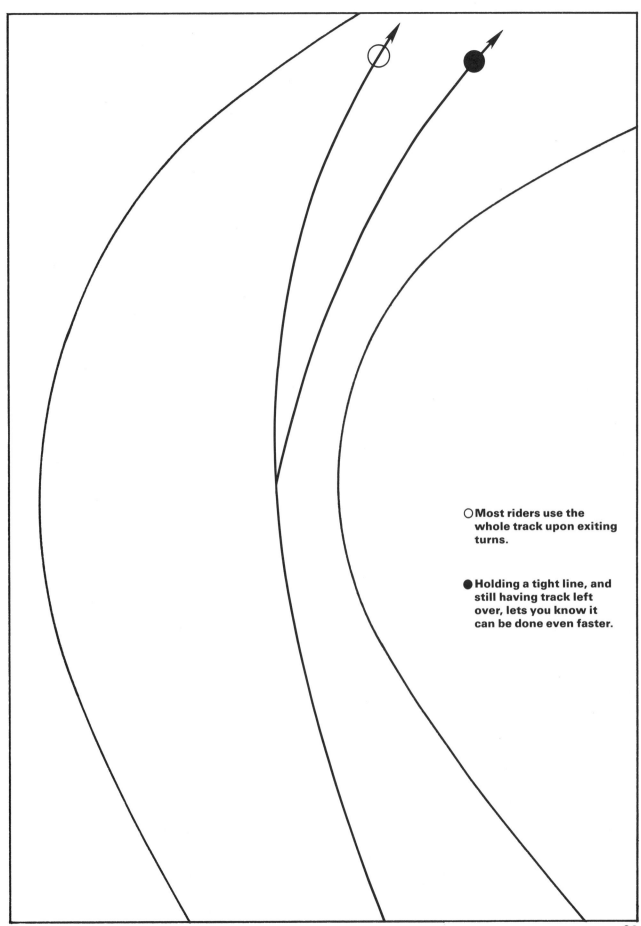

○ Most riders use the whole track upon exiting turns.

● Holding a tight line, and still having track left over, lets you know it can be done even faster.

CHAPTER FOUR

What You See

Programming Your Computer Through the Eyes

What you see through your smoke-tinted Bell shield has much to do with how well you ride. You can't count the number of objects you can see at any one spot on the track, any more than you can count what you see just staring at the back of your hand. The more you look, the more you see. This also applies to the race track. You can stop at any turn and look for hours at what's to be seen. But while you're racing or riding down the road, you can't stop to gaze.

How do you decide what to look at, what is important and what is not? And how do you use what you see? How can what you see help or hinder your riding? This chapter is about seeing correctly to improve your riding.

Where Are You?

The reason you look at points on the track is to learn where you are and where you are going. On any piece of road you look in front of you to obtain information about where you are so you can decide what to do with the information. Many riders have said, "You go where you look." What they failed to say is, "You can go where you don't look, but you roll off the throttle first." Let's restate it so the rider is more in control: **Look where you want to go.**

Reference Points

You use **reference points** to find out where you are on the track. **This point is a spot or object of which you already know the location.** It is something which clearly marks a place. You can refer to this object for information. Two **reference points** present a better picture of your location. Three or more give you your exact location. Example: you're looking for a store on Main Street. You go to Main Street—that's one **reference point.** You find the right block—that's two. You check the numbers to see which direction they run—that's three. You decide which side of the street the store is on—that's four. You follow the numbers till you reach the store. That's five or more **reference points** that you would use in finding an address. On a race track or road you do the same thing. **If you don't have enough reference points to know where you are—you're lost!** *Any examples?*

Reference Points (RPs)— a certain reminder of where you are; basic building blocks for your plan.

Reference points—yeah, you might not think about them but you've got to use them. Just little things on the track I remember—it helps to put it all together.

Things happen fast on a motorcycle at speed, and the situation changes constantly. Where you are on the road is very important because it determines your course of action. **If you don't know where you are, you also don't know what you're supposed to be doing.** Your location on a race track or road can be plotted in inches and feet—not in city blocks—and there are no street signs on the track. It's up to you to decide what **reference points** to use and what to do when you reach them. You must decide.

Familiar RPs allow you to look "around" the turn, well ahead of yourself.

An RP gives you information. It signals where, and how much, to change what you do.

What to Use as Reference Points

Your best Reference Point (RP) is something either on the track or very close to it: a patch of asphalt, a painted line, a spot, a crack, curbing, anything that doesn't move. Objects too far from the track surface will take your attention away from the track. Your RPs must be easy to find to be usable. At times you must use the edge of the track, but a point that's a foot in from the edge is better because it keeps your attention on the track. If you go to the limit with an RP that's one foot from the edge, you still have a foot left over. Going to the edge of the track means going to the limit and leaving yourself no margin for error. It isn't necessary to go to the edge of the track whenever possible until you feel comfortable doing so. The idea that you must use all the track is like the idea you must "hang off" the bike —only do it when it becomes necessary and comfortable.

The RPs you choose to look at should be in your line of vision and along your path of travel. Don't choose something as a reference point just because it's there and easy to see. It might not be the right RP for you because it's too far off your line or it doesn't work for the speed you're traveling. On the other hand, don't narrow your vision too much or you'll not have a wide enough view of the track surface to find where you are. RPs that are directly on your line of travel establish your location on the track lengthways. RPs along the side establish your location in relation to the width of the track. The bottom line for an RP is, **does it work?** It can be anywhere–so long as it works for you.

How to Use A Reference Point

A reference point is not merely something you can see easily on or near the track, **the reference point must mean something to you when you see it.** Every time you pass or approach it, this point must communicate a message to you, like, "This is where I begin looking for my turn marker," or "If I'm to the right of this too much I'll hit a bump, but to the left of it I'm alright." Or, "This is where I begin my turn." **Reference points are reminders of where you are or of what action you must take.** *Can you apply this?*

You'll need two or more **reference points** to accurately find yourself on the track. You've got to know where the RPs are so you can relate your own position to them. This may sound simple-minded, but if you narrow your attention to one object, it becomes your only RP and you become a victim of **target fixation.** You go to the RP because you don't have anything else to do. This occurs in a panic situation and can happen anywhere on a race track. You must have enough RPs so that target fixation doesn't occur.

When you have sufficient RPs in a turn or on the track, the scene moving in front of you appears to move smoothly, like a wide-screen 70mm movie. Too few and the scene looks like an old-time movie, bouncing and jerking along. Having only one RP is like watching a slide show frame—nice picture, but where do you go from there?

Having too few RPs causes target fixation. Enough RPs "open up" the track, making it appear larger, and costs less of your attention.

27

No doubt you've heard that you must look down the road where you're going, not where you are. This is good information—you need that second RP to locate yourself on the track. Looking too close to the bike won't help you find it.

Look Ahead for Reference Points

At 60 mph you're traveling at 88 feet per second; at 120 mph you're hurtling through space at 176 feet per second. That second ticks by very quickly, and if you're not ready for the next move, ahead of time, you'll make a mistake. Looking ahead for your **reference points** and **sub-products** gives you time to prepare for the next move so there are no surprises and so everything goes smoothly.

This idea can be taken too far, however. I've seen riders looking 150 feet down the road while rounding a tight 40-mph curve. They were ignoring what was to be seen in front of them, like curbing and holes. Still, other riders in the same turn were looking at the curbing and holes, but not until they were just 20 feet in front of them. Both of these extremes are unworkable; they produce uncertain riding through the turn and slow cornering.

Where to Look

Two factors will help you determine where to look while you're riding or racing.

1. At speed, the further ahead you look, the slower you believe you're going; the closer to yourself you look, the faster you believe you're going. **Look far enough ahead to avoid accelerating the scene, but not so far that you lose your feel for where you are on the track. With RPs you have a choice of where to look.** *Will you try it?*

2. Having enough RPs has the effect of **opening up the track, making it appear larger.** When you look too far ahead or too close to the bike, the track seems to narrow. If this begins happening, it is your signal to either change RPs or to find more of them in that turn or section of track.

These are guidelines. Adjust the RPs so the scene is moving at the right speed for you, and so you can see enough to keep the track "opened up."

Having only one RP is like having only one car. If it breaks or doesn't work, you don't go anywhere. If you have another you can easily use the one that works. With only one **reference point,** or car, it becomes too valuable and necessary. If you find that your attention is fixed on one point on the track or road, it's because you don't have another ready to use. That one becomes **very** valuable to you and you over-use it. You depend upon it for too much information and might begin staring at it. You can become slightly lost when it no longer lets you know where you are or what to do. If you find your attention becoming fixed on one RP, you need to find another in the area so the "movie" will smooth out.

Stepping Stones

Reference points are your stepping stones to the **products** and **sub-products** you will produce in a turn or series of turns. These little steps lead to the major changes you will make to get the bike around turns faster or with more confidence. RPs signal the points on the track where you will make these changes.

It's important to pick up good RPs, especially on the exit.

Concentration

On the track or road, concentration is a smooth flow, or chain of events that moves from one to another without a break. **Reference points** are parts of that chain, one link depending upon the next for strength and a continuous flow. If one link breaks, the entire chain stays broken until it can be repaired or replaced. If you have a section of the track with no, or too few RPs, your chain of concentration will break. **Reference points are the building blocks of concentration.**

Let's get back to the idea of your attention and how much of it you have, your ten-dollar bill. When your concentration is good, you spend just enough of it on each RP so that you know where you are and what to do. This keeps that steady flow going. When you have too few RPs in an area, most of your attention will be spent in trying to fix this bad situation. **The points or places on the track that you do not know, or understand, will occupy most of your attention.** Having enough RPs lets you spend just the right amount of time and attention on each one to get the information you need. You have enough left over to buy other things, to make small changes in your riding that will help you go just a bit faster or lean over just a bit more. **Everything you do on the track takes up some attention.** When you don't have enough RPs your attention goes right to that area and will—or can—break your concentration.

Some of the strangest things happen when you have a break in your concentration. One rider told me that every time his concentration breaks he begins thinking of a leaking faucet he has at home. Your mind may not wander to a leaking faucet, but when your concentration breaks you will notice that other things come into your mind. *Do you do this?*

Concentration—The Twist

There's a twist to this subject of concentration; when you've got it, it doesn't seem to you you're looking at anything in particular. The **reference points** just blend into the scene in front of you. When asked, "What do you look at in turns?" two or three of the top riders in the world have said, "I don't really look at anything." But is this really what they mean?

When your concentration is good, you spend just nickels and dimes on the RPs and none of them captures your attention. An example of this is that one major difference between riders is their ability to learn tracks. Learning a track means **knowing where you are on the track.**

I like to go to new tracks—it's fun. The first year I raced we went to the tracks that everybody raced and I just did OK. At the new tracks though, I was right there first or second.

Some riders can do it in five laps, others can't do it in 500 laps. Both guys have to learn where they are by **reference points;** the top riders just do it so fast they can beat you on your favorite road the second time you take them there!! One factor that separates the top riders from the rest of the field is that they pick up RPs quickly and accurately to the point they can see the "whole scene" without having to pick out the individual RPs.

Enough Reference Points

Once you have enough RPs, you can see the "whole scene" comfortably without having to stare at the RPs individually. This is your goal, and the individual building blocks of that scene are RPs. If your concentration becomes lost you will have to go back and rely on or relocate yourself with the RPs that are familiar to you.

That's how you restore your concentration as soon as possible: **Go back to the reference points you know and pick up the thread of concentration.** If you don't have any RPs in the area, it'll cost you time on the track as you hesitate and roll back the throttle.

Do Not Read Past This Next Paragraph Until You Have Completed the Experiment

Find a stopwatch or wall clock with a second hand and try this eye-opening experiment. Do it again after you have ridden the track looking for RPs.

1. Get a stopwatch.
2. Sit down in a comfortable chair.
3. Now, close your eyes and think of a race track you're familiar with. Start the watch and run through a complete lap on the track. Do it from memory. Try to go through it exactly as fast as you did the last time you rode there. You are timing your memory of the track and how you rode it.
4. Now, close your eyes and try it again.

Memory Lap

If you're like most riders, your memory "lap time" will be either much too long or much too short. If you just broke the absolute lap record by 20 or 30 seconds, or if you added 20 or 30 seconds to your actual lap times, it means the same thing—not enough **reference points.** The slow-lap rider's "movie" is incomplete and he finds himself star-gazing at the places he has no RPs. His attention is on the areas of the track he does not know.

In the very fast lap situation the rider still hasn't got enough RPs, so he flits from one to the next very quickly because those are what he does know. **Having sufficient RPs gives you a better sense of time because you now have points to mark your motion around the track.** Your attention goes either to the places you know very well, or to the place you don't know very well. Or, it becomes split between the two. This costs you a lot of attention you can't spend on other things.

Find the Lost RPs

Here's an easy method you can use to find out where you don't have enough RPs. You can use it anytime.

1. Close your eyes.

2. Carefully run through your own "movie" of the track as if you were riding.

3. "Ride" through one complete lap in your memory.

4. Open your eyes and draw each turn on a separate sheet of paper, marking the reference points you're sure of in each turn.

5. Make a note of what each RP means to you, like: "Braking Point," "Steering Change," "Location on the Track," "Bump," "Exit Marker," "Product," etc.

6. Close your eyes again and go back over your "movie," noticing the places you hesitate, go blank, where the scene gets foggy, or where you hurry through it too fast. Each of these situations indicates you have too few **reference points** at these locations.

7. Now make a note on your turn drawings at each place you have a blank spot or any other problem situation from No. 6 above.

8. Find more RPs for those areas the next time you ride the track.

You can use this method to find your weak spots—and strong points as well, as it is your memory of the turns you rely on when you ride. This is how you know where you're going. Knowing where you are going is part of the thread of concentration. *Will it work?*

That's the Twist

You must get to the point where you can see the whole scene in front of you without having to spend a lot of attention on any one point. You're building that scene with individual **reference points.** If your concentration is lost, go back to the RPs that you know and build the scene again.

The Big Twist to Concentration and Reference Points

A lot of guys I see out there seem to forget about the whole rest of the track. They are paying too much attention to that one line.

The trick to using RPs and gaining concentration is **you have to look at something.** Your eyes work by focusing on some object or some plane, then everything in that plane is in focus, like on a movie screen. You may be looking at only one area of the screen, but the entire screen is in focus.

Another point is that when your eyes move, they do so in short stopping movements. They flit from one object to another like a butterfly. If you try to sweep your eyes across a scene without stopping on anything, the scene becomes a blur. Try it.

A rider's problem is that he wants to see the track in front of him flowing as a whole scene, to maintain a steady flow of concentration, but his eyes don't work that way. If he stares at one **reference point** too long, he'll experience a form of tunnel vision. But because of the way his eyes work, he has to look at some specific thing! There's the twist.

Good RPs help keep a steady flow of concentration for a rider. You spend (use) RPs to save attention.

See Fast

How do the top riders manage to ride so fast without experiencing problems in seeing? Here's a drill that will help you practice the proper seeing techniques.

1. Find a wall that is entirely visible to you. You can see all four corners by moving your eyes, but not your head.

2. Focus your eyes on a spot in the middle of the wall.

3. Remain focused on that spot, then move your attention, not your eyes, to the upper right-hand corner of the wall.

Still focusing on that spot, move your attention to different places on the wall. You are looking at one spot but are aware of the other areas of the wall.

5. Still focusing on that spot, move your attention to the objects between you and the wall, and on the wall as well.

The Whole Picture

You can see the whole scene while still looking at one place or spot! You probably noticed that during this experiment you wanted to move your eyes from the spot you were focused on to the spot to which your attention had gone. This experiment becomes easier with practice. You can practice moving your attention around, while looking at one spot or area, as you're driving to the races or just sitting in a chair. It's a skill that can take time to develop if you haven't mastered it already.

Now, when you see the whole scene in this way you have to realize that the points in the scene must be well known to you. You need the **reference points** in the scene to make the scene. If you don't know the RPs your eyes will hunt for something that is familiar and lose the whole scene effect.

Being able to see the track in front of you as a whole scene makes riding much easier and brings your concentration back if it falters. As you can see in the drill above, it is where your attention is directed, where you're spending your ten-dollar bill, that's much more important than what you're looking at. Your attention must be spent economically, and looking at the whole scene rather than at one thing is spending it very wisely, and getting interest back on your investment. You just have to practice. *Will you try it?*

This is the way I see it most of the time—the overall scene. That's when things are going right—everything is working right.

You begin to understand a turn with RPs. Then pieces of the turn become clearer. Finally, the whole scene is viewed as a steady flow of action. You spend the least and get the most.

CHAPTER FIVE

Timing

Putting Things In Order

The first couple of practice laps feel fast, too fast, and then it slows down from there.

Timing really has nothing to do with your sense of time. It has to do with **taking the correct action at exactly the correct place on the track.** The whole idea of timing is to pull together your **reference points, products** and **sub-products** so they're useful to you on the track. Doing the correct thing at the wrong place on the track produces poor results. Knowing what to do, but not exactly where to do it, can really foul up a rider.

My Timing Lesson

I learned my lesson about **timing** from riding skateboards. I was trying desperately to make a "kick" turn, which is the 180-degree turn you make to get yourself back down after riding up a ramp or the side of a pool. I fell at least a hundred times trying it. Finally, I discovered that the board would not turn unless it was going at a certain slow speed. If I tried it too fast–too early–I could not make the turn. Too slow–too late–and the board would begin sliding backwards just enough to make the turn virtually impossible. There was a very fine margin of speed that would allow the board to be turned, yet still keep up the momentum so I could stay on and continue back down.

How You Let Off

I took a very close look at my motorcycle riding, keeping in mind what I'd learned on the skateboard, and discovered some very basic mistakes I was making as a rider. Many other riders were making the same mistakes for the same reasons.

In turns where you use the brakes, exactly where you let off them and when you begin steering can make a great difference in your smoothness. Though I could make that change in many different ways, one worked better than the others. Let's look at the possibilities:

1. You can finish the braking and then turn, leaving the throttle off.
2. You can finish the braking after you begin the turn, with no throttle.
3. You can finish the braking, then turn and apply the throttle.
4. You can finish the braking, and then crack the throttle slightly.
5. You can finish the braking after you begin to turn and apply the throttle.
6. You can finish the braking after you turn and just crack the throttle on.

What Happens

In Number One above, the forks are almost bottomed out from the braking, then when you let up on the brakes the forks extend and the bike "stands" up. You then put the bike into the turn, and the cornering forces compress the forks again. If you put it into the turn hard, the forks compress very far, then come back up a little. The bike is going up and down, changing traction and fork angle. That changes the steering and reduces the stability of the bike.

In Number Two above, the fork is down, and when you turn the throttle back on it comes up, then back down again from the turning forces. Here's the same situation again—loss of traction and stability.

In Number Three, the fork is compressed from the braking, then comes up when you release the brakes, then down again from the cornering loads, then up again as you apply the throttle. The other examples provide similar possibilities.

To get into the turn correctly, you must time the braking and turning so that the bike stays even, not going up or down, at the point you let off the brakes. You must let off the brakes at the exact moment your fork is compressed just enough for the speeds and cornering loads it will be undergoing through the turn. Apply the throttle so that fork extension doesn't change, or changes the least amount possible. This will allow you to go into the turn without any up and down motion. If your timing's off, you may complain that the bike handles poorly, possibly thinking the shocks are gone. *Some examples?*

Your Timing Target

Your target, or **sub-product** for any turn in which you brake and turn in succession, is **timing the braking, steering and throttle so that fork and shock extension are kept as even as possible.**

Fast "esses" and compound turns. When two or more turns are strung together and cannot be taken wide open, **timing** is important. On a quick right/left or left/right combination, time the steering change so that the throttle is rolled off right before the transition from side to side. Rolling off the gas just an instant before making the steering change dips the front end slightly, making the steering easier (oversteer) because of the decreased fork angle (rake). Making that steering change and compressing the suspension to its maximum point for that turn keeps the bike from bobbing up and down excessively. When done right, even a bike with poor shocks will handle fine. When done wrong, the best-handling bike in the world will handle poorly.

Roll-Off Time

The faster you ride, the harder the steering becomes, especially in high-speed "esses." Rolling the throttle off, then steering, then getting back on the gas again in the middle of two turns, can actually get you through faster than if you "push" through and have to roll off at the exit of the two turns. The rolling off and back on again should not take more than one second, and the gas is completely off for only a small fraction of that time, if at all. Avoid snapping the throttle on and off until your timing is perfect.

Tiredness = Loss of Timing

When you become tired, the first thing you lose is your timing. This is another reason it's so important to have your **reference points** and **products** well established. **Sub-products,** the major steps or changes in a turn, are also **points of timing (POT).**

Not all RPs are **points of timing.** Some only tell you where you are, signaling an upcoming change or **POT/sub-product.** If you know where they are and what to do there, you won't have to slow down as much when you become tired. You probably won't be willing to go faster, but that can wait until you're sharp again. *Does this apply to you?*

Timing and the Road You Ride

Changes in the road affect **timing** dramatically. You not only have to work the controls correctly, but you have to fit that into the camber changes and radius changes as well. For instance, if you were coming up to a banked turn where you would have to use the brakes first, you should know that the suspension will compress more in that turn than it will on a similar turn that is flat with no banking. To go in perfectly, you would let off the brakes as you go into the banking just as the suspension is taking the load from the centrifugal force. This will give you the smoothest entry. **You back out of the brakes just as the turn takes over the job of compressing the suspension.** If you brake too hard and the cornering speed is down, the bike will rise up when you hit the banking, the suspension will unload. If you get off the brakes too soon and then hit the banking, the suspension will compress. The second of these is the better of the evils as it offers a better traction situation. Doing it right, of course, is best of all.

In off-camber turns:
1. Spend as little time in them as possible.
2. Design your plan around the forces pulling you to the outside of the turn.

Off-Camber Timing

In an off-camber turn it is better to have the bike as light as possible on its wheels to keep it from moving to the outside of the turn too much. You must time your control operations so you're on the gas the least amount in that part of the turn. Traction deteriorates rapidly in off-camber sections, compared with flat or banked sections. Rolling off the throttle very hard in an off-camber has an effect similar to that of rolling on too hard. It loads one wheel more than the other—in this case the front—and can cause the front end to slide out. The rider might be puzzled—he rolled off the throttle and still threw it away. Rolling off usually helps him get through turns when he's been going too fast. Keeping the weight even on the wheels by cracking open the throttle, not accelerating or slowing, gives the bike its best traction in off-camber turns. In an off-camber, set up your POT so the bike is accelerating or slowing the least amount possible. That will prevent transferring too much weight to either wheel.

Changing the Track with Timing

In a section of track where a dip compresses the suspension, it is sometimes possible to time your roll-on for that point. Ground clearance increases when the bike is accelerating because the suspension is extending; this tactic may stop some of the bobbing up and down that occurs in dipped parts of the track. **Timing** can change the track conditions for better or worse. If you get the POT right it can work—if you don't, it won't.

Products and Timing

Keep in mind through all this that your goal is still the overall **product** of the turn. You still want the maximum speed, the drive coming out, or you want to be set up for the next turn. If you make parts of the turn work, but lose the drive coming out, you've won the battle but lost the war. All of the RPs and **POT/sub-products** must make the product better or you have done a lot of fancy riding that's slow riding. Sometimes it's better to go directly through a rough section of track wobbling and out of shape than to figure a smoother—but slower—way around it. Your measure of progress is in whether or not your **product** is improving.

Points of timing are sub-products, and this is where changes are made. Every place where you take any kind of action is a **point of timing,** especially when you're in a turn. Upshifting on the straight-away, for instance, is a POT, though it's less important than where you steer in a turn. Becoming familiar with your POT and **products** allows you to loaf on the rest of the track because now you understand where you have to work hard and where you don't. If you get these facts down on paper, or well memorized, you won't be saying things like, "I'm having trouble in the esses." You'll see which POT are working and which are fouling up your **product.** *What will change if you do this?*

Timing in Perspective

To put **timing** in perspective, let's look at Turn Six at Riverside Raceway in Riverside, California. It's a good example because hundreds of riders are still baffled by it, and it's the most complex turn I know of.

Each change in the track requires the rider to adjust his bike at exactly the right place. If not, the bike will seem to handle poorly.

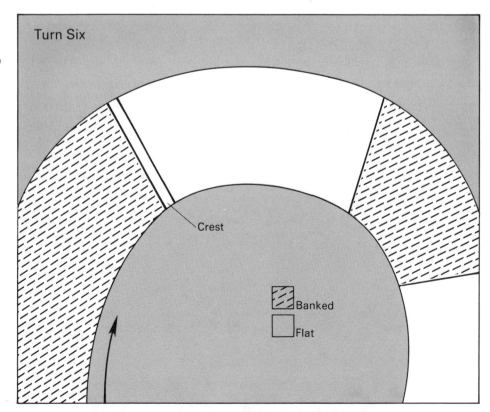

Turn Six

Crest

Banked

Flat

Turn Six, Riverside

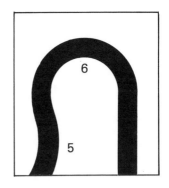

Turn Six is part of a series beginning with Turn Five (see diagram). Turn Five is faster than Six, and most riders brake and go down a gear coming into Five. It looks very narrow on the approach, but as they're coming out of it, most riders find they've gone through it too slow. The gas comes on for an instant as they ride up the hill into Turn Six, where they have to use the brakes again. Most riders overuse the brakes here, find they're going a bit too slow, then jump on the gas again. Just at that point, it seems the gas is on too much again, so they roll it off. Now it seems too slow again, so they get back on the gas. Now they see the end of the turn, but the bike's heading to the outside too fast, aiming for the dirt and the Armco barrier. Here's another roll-off. Now the bike's on the straight-away and back onto the gas. This is a rough way to go through a turn!

Here's what happened—coming into Turn Six, the rider first notices that he has overbraked and is going too slow because he has failed to see that the track is banked at this point. Now he has the advantage of the banking, but just when he begins to roll on, the track flattens out and he loses the banking. The new roll-on begins where the track picks up the banking again about two-thirds of the way through. The final roll-off begins where the banking goes away again at the exit of the turn. That's four camber changes in one turn!

Other factors affect this turn. At the beginning, where we lose the first banking and the roll-off begins, there is a crest on the track. Not only does the banking taper off, but the bike becomes light as it goes over this crest. The suspension unloads, traction goes away and the bike wants to go toward the wall—very fast!

The bike settles down at the banked part of the exit and the rider feels he is going too slow again. Now it takes time for him to notice that the traction is better here and time to get back on the gas again. By then, the banking begins to go away at the exit and the bike is going too fast. The last roll-off occurs. The additional twist to that last part of the turn is that it tightens up and goes downhill a bit.

This turn has four camber changes, two radius changes, two elevation changes and a hump in the middle of the first camber change! To make it worse, the pavement's poor. The track designer must have really had fun with this turn.

Find the Timing

There is nothing really wrong with riders rolling on and off the throttle. The problem is they're not doing it at the right place on the track. Their **timing** is all wrong. This is because, first of all, they have not looked at the track and found where it changes. Remember, you cannot see these changes very well when you're riding. Secondly, no **points of timing** are established to signal the changes. As a result, the braking and throttle responses to the track occur in the wrong place. Third, they establish no plan to take advantage of the banking. Use the rule of thumb that the bike should be at the lowest point of the banking when leaving it. Fourth, no overall **product** has been determined from previous experience.

My description of riders going through Turn Six might sound like bad drama, but watching them is worse. Their worried expressions and frozen attitudes tell the whole story. Their bikes bob up and down from the throttle changes as if their shocks were broken. After riding Turn Six like this a while, you can begin to feel very stupid. As a result, many riders choose a constant-radius line and pretend it's all just one turn with no real camber or radius changes.

Riders take this turn many different ways, but the fastest ones consistently do three things: 1) They use the banking going into the turn to maximum advantage. 2) Rather than trying to fight the middle of the turn, where it flattens out, they let the bike drift out, which allows them to take advantage of the following point. 3) They use the banking on the exit to its best advantage. This line could basically be called a double apex, which is a good description of the turn. Keep in mind that the timing must be correct for it to work right.

Turns with fewer changes can be equally baffling, if the **timing** is wrong. Some riders, of course, can go through this turn very fast by keeping up a fever pitch of concentration and cat-like reflexes, but they won't be as fast as someone who understands it. And riding at, or past, your concentration redline wears you out sooner. *Are you aware of this?*

Shaving the Track

You don't have to keep up a razor edge of concentration everywhere on the track. You've still got that ten dollars worth of attention you're trying to spend wisely. If you continue spending all of it all the time, you'll soon use it up. Spending the whole ten dollars to go down the straight is a waste. Put it in savings to draw interest in attention-saving, then withdraw it again for the next turn.

Your attention and ability to concentrate come and go; they're better at some times than at others. **By spending your attention only when necessary, it will be there when you need it.** This is another part of **timing,** recognizing where you have to do the tight work, and cooling it the rest. At six-hour endurance races I have heard a number of

riders say they were pacing themselves to last the whole race by trying to relax—and they went quicker than they had in the sprint races! They forced themselves to get smart. If you can use this attitude for sprint races, you can be even sharper when you have to be. Just figure where your POT are and what you're supposed to be doing at each one. Relax while going down the straight—it's fun to go fast. Set up a **reference point** to tell you when to start paying attention. Make it work for you. You can always set up a RP to signal you that a POT is coming, and this will help you relax. Get ready when you see it, not before.

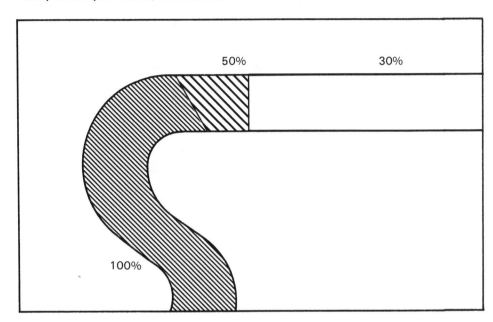

50%   30%

100%

Spend attention when necessary but save it where you can.

Rhythm = Timing

Riders talk about the rhythm of a race track or piece of road, of getting the flow of the road. This is **timing**. The rider is fitting himself and his equipment into the track and all the actions he has to take on it. The basis of **timing** is understanding—not super-fast reflexes. **Fast reflexes are not a substitute for good timing.** At the speeds attained on a road-race track, good or even incredible reflexes don't win races. If you plan to go road racing because you have fast reflexes, figure out how long you have to make a change at 180 mph when you're traveling at 264 feet per second! There is no substitute for understanding on a race track. You've got to have **RPs, POT, sub-products** and **products** to guide you around. Fast reflexes help, but **timing** is the key that unlocks the mysteries of the asphalt.

Note: Some of the problems of timing that are part of going into a turn have been helped by the various anti-dive devices now available on street bikes and more widely applied to GP racing machines and superbikes.

Timing Involves Both an Idea and an Action

You must understand both the track and your own actions so you're not fighting each other. Do this by knowing what to do and where to do it. I'm sure you can look back over your riding and recall situations where, because your **timing** was off, you experienced uncomfortable situations. The second part is in going out and actually doing it. Get the **timing** right first, then add speed.

If your timing is right you can make it smooth. If I make a change just before the main event and it doesn't work out, I just have to make it work with good timing.

CHAPTER SIX

Decisions

Decision-Making: Recipe for Skill

I'm always talkin' to myself out there on the track. I can get outside of myself and look at what I'm doing and sometimes, if what is going on isn't just right, I get mad at myself.

The act of riding a motorcycle amounts to putting a whole string of **decisions into motion.** Every movement you make on a bike is based upon a **decision** you have made in the past, or are making as you ride. **You don't do anything automatically or without making a decision.** For example, again, some riders say they shift gears "automatically" without thinking about it. That's not true. They may spend only a nickel or a dime of their attention on this decision, but they're spending something.

If you study it, you'll see that many little **decisions** go into making one gear change. You **decide** when the engine is spinning at the right rpm. You **decide** how fast to make the gear change. You may **decide** that one place is better than another to shift, and how much throttle to apply when you turn it on again. None of these things is "automatic," but once you have made a **decision,** it costs you less attention to do it. That's the magic of **decisions.**

Decisions in motion. Eddie Lawson's flawless style is the result of hundreds of correctly made decisions. Making decisions puts you in control.

You Must Make a Decision

At all times you're operating upon **decisions,** whether they're past or present. For example, you can let out the clutch in several ways. If you're familiar with these different methods, you <u>still</u> must decide which to use. You still must make a **decision.**

You can arrive at a **decision** in two ways. One is to work at the problem until you have narrowed it down by the process of elimination, or Trial and Error **(T&E).** In the above example, this is how we learn to clutch our bikes. The second method of arriving at a **decision** is to <u>think</u> through the task, then make the **decision.** We'll call this method Thinking It Through **(TIT).**

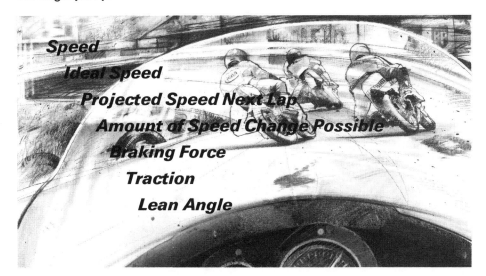

Speed
Ideal Speed
Projected Speed Next Lap
Amount of Speed Change Possible
Braking Force
Traction
Lean Angle

Decisions are the details of your overall "plan." Making a decision gives you a place to start, and something to change, or stop, if it doesn't work out.

T & E

The first method, Trial and Error, or **T&E,** depends less upon understanding and more upon practice. You don't think through the problem, you keep performing the action till it works. If you come up with the correct method, you're alright. But the drawback to making **decisions** by **T&E** is that if you change them, you must go through the whole process again to find another way. Really good riders who learned by **T&E** have gone through the many possible methods of riding a motorcycle so often that they can use any of them at will. They have an entire mental library of **T&E** decisions to draw on.

TIT

Method Two, **Think It Through.** or **TIT,** also has drawbacks. **To arrive at a correct decision you must start with correct information.** The rider has to be a good observer, he has to review the information from the last ride, and it has to be correct and useful information. A wild example would be to **decide** to go through Turn One at Daytona wide open in sixth gear. A person who learns by **T&E** probably wouldn't make such a mistake. The "thinker," of course, would only make that mistake once. *Can you see it working for you?*

A Drawback

The serious drawback to Thinking It Through is in making decisions based upon other people's information. One rider tells another to ride in a certain way, then the second rider goes out and tries to fit his riding style into what he was told. If the information is accurate it can work. For example, a rider told me the reason my left arm was cramping was because I was using the clutch for upshifts, which isn't necessary. I stopped using it to upshift and my arm no longer cramped. This was great—it worked!

Another example of this, and a grim one, was when one rider told another he could go over the crest of Turn Seven at Riverside with the bike flat out in fifth gear. Actually, it's a 60-mph turn. The rider went over the crest at more than 100 mph on his first lap. . . . Need I say what happened?

A proper balance of "Thinking It Through" (TIT) and "Trial and Error" (T & E) can eliminate many mistakes.

The Best Approach

A combination of the two methods, Trial and Error (T&E) and Thinking It Through (TIT), is the best approach to decision making. T&E is time-consuming. Unless you're a full-time factory-contracted racer you may find it difficult to regularly go riding or to rent time on a race track. You've got to make every trip to the track count, and that means you must return from every session with information that will be usable for the TIT method. Laps on a race track will do nothing but wear out your equipment if you don't take accurate information home so you'll have a clear picture of **what decisions you have made and what to do in the future.** Will this help?

44

T & E Only

A rider who uses the T&E method only cannot work on his riding when he is off the track. He can't work out new **decisions** on how to ride faster because he doesn't have the information stored in himself. T&E riders face another disadvantage. **Life sometimes throws upsets at us that go with us out on the track.** These upsets can consume vast quantities of **attention**—usually more than we can spare. When T&E riders are upset they have an "off" day. Some things that happen can affect one's whole life, including the ability to make decisions. TIT-method riders are less affected by what happens off the track because their **decisions** are based on what they understand.

Real-World Riding

Let's leave the world of ideas for a time and return to the real world of riding to see how the decisions we make can affect us on the road or track. Take braking for example. The overuse of the rear brake is the one braking **decision** that commonly turns out the worst. When most riders learn to ride, they learn that the rear brake can stop the motorcycle. They **decide** it will do that. They know the front brake will also stop the bike, but while they're learning in a parking lot or street it's upsetting when the front end of the bike dives down every time they use the front brake. They decide at that time, right from the start, that the rear brake is better.

Now, even after a rider is told to use the front brake, the rear will be his first choice because he has already made the decision the rear is better. Studies of motorcycle accidents have concluded that in most cases, when a rider is trying to avoid an accident he uses only the rear brake. He may know the front brake will stop him much quicker, but that original **decision** is so strong in an emergency that down go the bike and rider. **In an emergency, a rider will do what he has already decided will work.** In this case, and possibly many others, what he decided was incorrect for that situation. *Does this apply to you?*

Changing Decisions

In order to change a **decision** that doesn't work, and that has become a bad habit, you must **go back to the original decision and un-learn it.** Maybe "un-learn" is not correct—actually, you're making a new decision after the old one has been identified and thrown out. **You don't make a new decision over the old one, you erase the first decision before making another.**

In racing, you are creating an almost continuous emergency situation by pushing to your limits. The same sort of thing applies in emergencies. The rider performs an action that has appeared to work in the past in similar situations.

Not knowing causes and effects creates the opposite of **decisions—that is, in-decision.** In an emergency, **indecision** can be very costly. If you don't understand the front brake's limits, you'll spend a lot of attention using it. That's because you know the front brake does the best job of slowing and stopping (that **decision** has already been made), but you don't know at what point it will lock up and cause you to fall. This creates **indecision.** Once a rider learns at what point the front brake locks up, and what to do about it, he can make clear-cut **decisions** on how to use it.

Another decision-making myth is that a rider can figure out his lines by studying a track diagram. It's impossible to **decide** how to ride a race track or piece of road before you have actually seen it. Studying a track diagram at that point is useless. Trying to fit a track diagram into the real world of riding, while you're still trying to learn the track, will only take your attention away from the real job. *Do you agree?*

Make It Happen

Deciding to do something is the first step to making it happen. You can make lots of **decisions,** but making too many of them will confuse you. Start with the important decisions first. Find Reference Points, Points of Timing, Sub-Products and Products, then **decide** how they fit together with the track. You put it together by **deciding** how it's going to be done, then you do it. Of course, you must have a very accurate understanding of the track changes. That includes knowing the location of the camber changes and radius changes. All the information from Chapter One, "The Road You Ride," must be gathered first. Always look at the track and remember that the man who designed it was trying to fool you into making poor **decisions.**

Deciding How

Deciding how to ride a track by looking it over does not always work, especially if you aren't riding it. After riding California's Sears Point once, I walked the track to find out what I could learn. I laid on the ground and looked at each turn from the beginning, then walked through and looked at it backwards. I stood in the middle. I got up on the hills. I looked at every turn from the inside out. As I was doing this, I was figuring the "ideal" line through each turn.

During practice I rode it just as I had decided it should be ridden. I went three seconds slower than I had the last time at the track. It didn't work. The "ideal" line doesn't take into account bumps, sliding and speed.

I went back to riding it the way I had **decided** to from my earlier ride. My lap times were now two seconds faster than I had ever gone before, and five seconds faster than my "ideal" line. I had learned that a combination of T&E and TIT is the key to success.

You can't have one without the other, but it's important to first **decide** how to do it, then **decide** why it did or did not work. It isn't just blind experimenting, but a firm **decision** to do it one way, doing it that way no matter how it feels, then learning the results by looking at the lap times. *Should it be tried?*

Lap Times

Lap times are your most reliable method of deciding what works. You simply **decide** what to do, then go out and do it. This means **deciding** where your **Points of Timing, Products** and **Reference Points** are, then **deciding** what you'll do in this practice session, then reviewing your lap times to **decide** if it worked or not. Did these changes improve your lap times? Did the lap times stay the same, but you found it easier to ride at this level? Both of these conclusions are valuable. **When you become comfortable with the decisions at one level of riding, you can move on to the next level.**

Lap times must be the basis for your **decisions** because any other method can fool you too easily. In most cases, riders will do what feels right, but what feels right is not always the quickest way around the track or down the road. I learned another thing from my Sears Point "ideal" line adventure. You can be going faster in the entrance and middle sections of a turn, but can sacrifice a good drive on the exit because of it. Getting out of the turn with a one- or two-mph faster **product** will make a great difference on the next straight. A good speed through the center of the turn, but a poor drive, will be worse for lap times. It's easy to fool yourself this way. Here are three points to consider: **1) Good decisions result in good lap times. 2) Good lap times are those that improve and can be done consistently. 3) Lap times are a reflection of the quality of the rider's decisions.** *Any notes?*

Go Faster

There is, of course, a twist to the **decision-making** game which has to do with how powerful a **decision** can be. Sometimes a rider simply **decides** to go faster. He will apply this overall **decision** to his riding and–bang!–his lap times come down just like that! It can happen for many different reasons. Watching other riders going faster can sometimes change your mind about how fast you can ride. You **decide** you can do it, too. **Deciding** to beat a quicker rider can spark new life into tired lap times.

But **deciding** to go faster without gaining enough experience from either T&E or TIT can get you into trouble. Often, after a day's race, you can hear racers talking about all the places they can make up time. "I know I can go a lot faster in Turn Three and Turn Nine." The pit racers are cutting record laps by the hundreds! Beating your own performance is one of the great rewards of racing, but be careful. Decide to go faster only when you've had enough experience to back it up. Simply **deciding** to cut better lap times in practice may not work if you don't know where you're going to pick up that time. **Work out the decisions that will back up an overall decision to go faster.** *Can you do it?*

Often times, when a baby learns to walk, he **decides** to run after he's taken his first few steps. The run usually lasts about three steps; in a racer's case, maybe three laps. Other sweeping **decisions** that usually work out rather poorly are: "I'm going to out-brake him, no matter what," and "I'll shut down later than he does." At 120 mph, later is a long way down the road.

Past Decisions

To ride a motorcycle, you must draw on your past **decisions,** and on your ability to make **decisions** in the present. The **decisions** you make determine how well your riding will go. The rider's job is to sort out the decisions he is using to get around the track, to know them and to change them when necessary. The **decisions** can be simple ones like using less rear brake to prevent wheel hop while going into a turn, or timing your entrance to a turn so the bike doesn't undergo a lot of up and down suspension movement. The **decisions** can be harder to find and correct. Having trouble going into turns too soon, a common error, might be based on the **decision** "not to go in high or wide," rather than the **decision** "to go in low or tight."

You see, this can be very tricky. A rider could spend a lot of time trying to **decide** how to enter a turn, trying to figure out another way to do it. He discovers he is always going in low, so he thinks that he has decided to go low. His real **decision** , way back when, was "I don't want to go in too high because it's unsafe." So he now **decides** to go higher against that earlier **decision** not to go higher. When he tries to use the higher line he runs into a resistance, which is like a mental wall, telling him not to do it. His earlier **decision** has made it very uncomfortable for him to change. A **decision** can be very powerful if you don't understand it.

Every once in a while you might discover one of these past decisions and think, "Hey, I can do that! Whatever made me think I couldn't?" When you change your earlier **decision,** you can suddenly make a great breakthrough in your riding. You have to realize when you have made a false **decision,** then put a better, more workable one in its place. *Some examples?*

Discover Your Decisions

The **decisions** you make while riding are based upon the past **decisions** you've made, whether they were made recently or a long time ago. Here's a way to **discover your decisions.**

1. Think over your actions on a particular turn or track situation. Do this for sections that are going well, and for those that are giving you trouble.

2. Evaluate how well your actions work.

3. How clear are all the steps involved in this action?

4. What standard tells you how well you're doing or going?

5. What decisions have you made to help you reach your goals,

or what decisions are keeping you from reaching them?

      6. Should you decide to:

        A. Change the **decision?**

        B. Not change it?

        C. Check again to see what **decisions** you have already made?

        D. Or, look for more information before making a new **decision?**

In each item you come up with in 1 through 6 above, you may also ask:

1. How is my timing?

2. What are my **Points of Timing?**

3. What **Reference Points** do I use?

4. What is my **Product?**

5. How much **attention** am I spending?

      You can do this for each turn of the track. It will take you a long time, and it isn't easy to do, but it will help. Also, it's cheaper than tires and engines.

Some Decisions About Braking

      The following is a partial list of decisions you could make about using the brakes. They are not of equal importance, but each of them involves a potential **decision.**

      Take a look at each one. Consider each very seriously by applying it to a situation you've been in. Or, you can just look them over for reference and be aware of them.

      If you have the time over the long winter months, you may even make your own lists of other aspects of riding. Take another, like steering or throttle control, and break it down into the decisions and actions you must make while riding.

      Here are 104 possible decisions that you have made or can make concerning the use of brakes. Some of them are more important than others and some cover the same ground in a slightly different manner. Look them through and reflect back upon your riding with these in mind. You may be able to think of other decisions that apply to the use of brakes. Just looking over this list and thinking over these decisions can help improve your braking.

How many fingers to use for the front brake
How much lever pressure it takes to lock up the front brake
How much lever pressure it takes to lock up the rear brake
How hard you can use the front brake going into slow turns
How hard you can use it braking into fast turns
How hard you can use it braking into medium-speed turns
How hard you can use it braking into a series of turns
How hard you can use the brakes in the first turn of a series
How hard you can brake going into the second turn of a series
Braking in downhill sections

Braking in uphill sections
Braking into a banked section
Braking into a flat corner
Braking into an off-camber turn
Braking into a decreasing-radius turn
Braking into an increasing-radius turn
Braking into a constant-radius turn
Braking on a smooth surface
Braking on a choppy surface
Braking into right-hand turns
Braking into left-hand turns
Braking on crested roads
Where you should be on the track as you begin to brake
Where you should be on the track during braking
Where you should be on the track at the end of the braking *Some examples?*

More Decisions

What you look for that tells you when to begin braking (in each kind of turn)
What you look for that tells you when to end the braking (in each kind
    of turn)
(The above two questions can be applied to particular tracks)
Timing your braking going into slow turns
Timing your braking going into medium-speed turns
Timing your braking going into fast turns
Timing your braking going into a series of turns
Timing your braking on downhill sections
Timing your braking on uphill sections
Timing your braking on banked track
Timing your braking on flat track
Timing your braking on off-camber track
Timing your braking in decreasing-radius turns
Timing your braking in increasing-radius turns
Timing your braking in constant-radius turns
Timing your braking in constant-speed turns
Timing your braking on smooth surfaces
Timing your braking on choppy surfaces

Still More Decisions

What **Points of Timing** or **Reference Points** do you use to tell if the
    braking is going well?
What **POT** or **RP** do you use to decide the location of your beginning
    braking point?
What **POT** or **RP** do you use to decide the location of your end braking
    point?
What information do you use to decide if the braking began early enough?
What information do you use to decide if the braking started too late?
What information do you use to decide if the braking started on time?

Decisions With Practice

Braking over discolored or changing pavement surface
Using the rear brake in conjunction with the front
Using the rear brake only
Using the front brake only
What to do when the rear end begins to hop or slide
How to correct rear-wheel hop or slide
Locking up the front brake
Locking up the front and rear brakes together
Other people's information on the use of brakes in general
Other people's information on the front brake
Other people's information on the rear brake
Other people's information on using both brakes together
Information you got from watching other riders use the brakes
What is useful to do with the brakes
What is not useful to do with the brakes
Braking when the bike is straight up
Braking when the bike is leaned over
Braking with only the front brake while leaned over
Braking with only the rear brake while leaned over
How far you can be leaned over and still use the brakes
Braking and steering at the same time
How good is your braking overall?
How much time can be made up with brakes?
How much distance you can make on another rider by using your brakes
Your seating position while braking

A critical moment of decision. How much brake to use while leaned over?

Use of throttle and brake at the same time
How slowly or quickly you can let off the front brake
How slowly or quickly you can let off the rear brake
How to judge your speed at the end of the braking action
Where to position the brake lever
Where to position the brake pedal
How much stopping force the front brake has
How much stopping force the rear brake has
How much stopping force the front and rear brakes have together
How much the lever and pedal pressure can be changed while braking

More Decisions With Practice

Where to put your weight while braking
Putting your weight on the handlebar while braking
Putting your weight on the footpegs while braking
Putting your weight on the tank while braking
Sitting up while braking
Hanging off while braking
Braking and downshifting at the same time
Passing while using the brakes
What happens to the steering geometry during braking
What happens to weight transfer during braking
What happens to the suspension during braking
How much attention you spend beginning braking
How much attention you spend during braking
How much attention you spend at the end of braking
Which is the most important part of braking–beginning, middle or end
How much front brake can be used if the rear is locked up
How good is your sense of traction while braking
How good is your sense of speed while braking
How good is your depth perception while braking
Your ability to improve your braking *Will this help?*
Phew!!

What Decisions Have You Made About Racing?

CHAPTER SEVEN

Barriers

Keys to Improvement

Barrier: Anything serving as a limitation or obstruction. A barrier obstructs but is not impassable. While riding and racing, you'll constantly confront barriers to your going faster. Your goal is to lower your lap times by riding around the track at higher speeds and with more control. Riders hit levels of lap times that act as barriers, however, and they can become stuck there. Ideally, you would be able to ride a little faster and improve your average lap time each time you returned to a track. That would be a good target for you to consider, and a real goal to set for yourself.

Time Barriers

When you begin trying to go faster, you will notice that things also happen a lot faster. You have less time between corners, between Reference Points, and there's less time to make decisions. You have created this emergency situation by adding speed, and by compressing your time to act. If you're able to cope with this change, your lap times will improve. But if you have to put yourself into **panic reaction time,** you may learn nothing by the extra speed—except what it feels like to panic.

Having less time to make your decisions is not necessarily bad, for it is one of the indicators that you've increased your speed. Whenever you reach one of these time **barriers** you're knocking on the door of your next area to conquer. A riding **barrier** is useful because it's telling you that you need to make new decisions faster. **It is your automatic instructor.** You don't need to find a new line through a turn—you need to figure out what factors are bringing you near panic, then control them. These **barriers** are like warning lights on the dashboard of your car. If you handle each one as it appears, you'll avoid a catastrophe later. *Where does this apply?*

A Riding Barrier Signals an Area That Needs Improvement

You can recognize these problem areas in several ways. The first is that you're being pressed to react a little beyond your abilities.

You're not being pushed completely beyond your ability, but enough that your attention is fixed upon the problem. An example is that you're entering a turn and the braking and downshifting are crowded so close to the steering action that you're unable to accurately pick a good **Point of Timing** to act without being absolutely frantic. If you're snapping and grabbing at the controls like a shark at feeding time, you know something isn't right.

In this example, many problems could be affecting your approach. Here are some possibilities. A lack of good **Reference Points** can cause that kind of panic that occurs when you're slightly lost. Or you may simply be downshifting too late and crowding it into your other actions. You may be going down one gear too many and have your atten-

Track barriers, or problem areas, are places where your riding is "soft." You are either late and have to panic, or are waiting for something to happen. What you are doing is definitely unclear.

tion stuck to an engine spinning at 13,000 rpm when it should be on turning. You may be braking so late that you're losing sight of your entry speed, resulting in a panic situation. The controls on your bike may be set at such an uncomfortable angle that you can't reach them quickly.

The track construction itself may contribute to your distress. For example, the entrance may be off camber or downhill, and offers less potential braking than a flat surface. You may not have a **product** for the turn and that will bother you. You may not know where you're going. Of the many possible problems in approaching a turn, these are just a few.

Other Clues

Besides being pressed for time to act, other clues will tell you you're not on top of the situation. A feeling of uncertainty comes from not fully understanding your situation. It could stem from one of the above reasons or from many others. Whatever the reason, the uncertainty will eat up your attention—attention that could well be spent elsewhere for a higher return. This is another **barrier.**

Go over your decisions. First year road racer, Wayne Rainey, thinking it through just moments before his first National Superbike win at Loudon.

Mistakes

Another great indicator that all is not well is when you make mistakes on the track. When you make a mistake, find out where your attention was focused just before it happened. Look at the decision leading up to the mistake, as it's always the last thing you do that gets you into trouble. Remember, **a mistake is a result, not a cause.** This is why you must always know **what you do** and be able to remember it in detail. Mistakes aren't all that valuable—it's in remembering what you did to bring them about that will help you correct them. **A mistake isn't to be**

ignored in the hope it will disappear with practice—it is something to be studied and figured out. It is a **barrier** to improvement, and therefore a key to improvement if handled correctly.

Feeling Like You Can't Do It

This is very frustrating to a rider, and it creates trouble for him. This helpless feeling often results from not knowing the track layout well enough, or from not being in full control of the bike in some situations. If you can't handle counter-steering in a turn, you might begin to believe it can't be done the way it looks. The worst problem with this feeling is that you may decide it can be done because someone else is doing it, then you try to do it before you have the skill necessary. You berserk it. This dangerous condition results from frustration, and it's another indicator of a **barrier** to your riding.

Overcoming your barriers is not impossible—it just takes some work. You can do the work at the track, in between riding sessions or races. First, draw yourself pictures of each turn, then go through them, marking down the spots where you're having difficulty or making mistakes. Close your eyes and go over the turns in your mind as you try to find the problem areas (see Chapter Four—"What You See"). As you're studying the track from memory, some parts will be foggy, unclear or just not there. Mark down these spots on your turn diagrams. Go over the entire track by memory and mark all the places that are barriers to you, whether they're caused by uncertainty, rushed time, mistakes or other problems.

The Barriers Change

Once you have listed your barriers, go back over them and decide how you can change your riding to overcome them. Remember, **the barriers will change as you go faster.** There is a twist to barriers. Don't overlook the possibility that the same problems can occur again, even in the same turn, as you increase your speed.

Overall, **barriers** are good things. They tell you automatically where your problems lie. They are saying, "This is your next area to expand into, your next level of improvement." Welcome it when you notice that something's not going right. Once you recognize your barriers, you won't have to guess what's keeping your lap times down—they will point to your problems. It's free instruction! *Will you remember this?*

Look for the other indicators that there is some riding barrier slowing your progress.
1. Mistakes.
2. Feeling helpless or like you can't do it.
3. Pressed for time to act.
4. Doing nothing, waiting for something to happen.
5. Can't get a clear picture of some turn or area.
6. Attention stuck on some part of the track.

Remember, the track is what you have to beat. You don't beat other racers, you beat the track better than they did.

Break the track into portions—turns, or parts of a turn. Pay particular attention to the places you are unsure of.

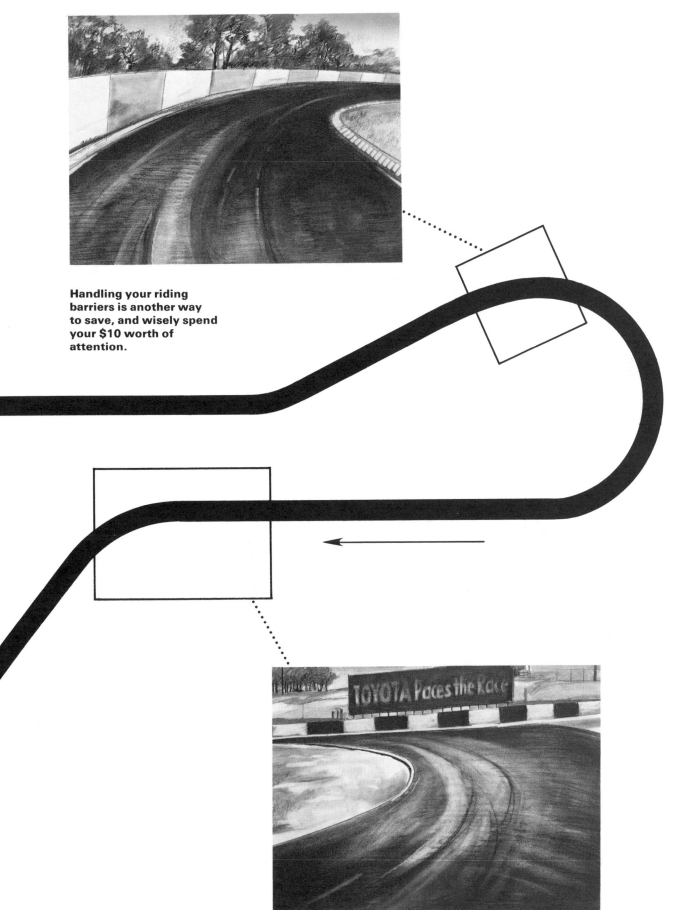

Handling your riding barriers is another way to save, and wisely spend your $10 worth of attention.

CHAPTER EIGHT

Braking

The Art of Regulating Speed

Motorcycle brakes have undergone many major technical breakthroughs since the advent of the disc brake, and they have become extremely efficient. Brake technology has surpassed most other technologies, such as suspension, for instance. You can buy a set of brakes that would stop a car, and install them on your bike in an afternoon. Tuning your suspension, however, can be an endless and painstaking task. This chapter will discuss the purpose of brakes in high-performance riding and racing, their limits, and what you should know about the business of braking.

The Most Important Factor

The single most important factor to be aware of in braking is the weight transfer that occurs when the brakes are applied. Let's say you have a 450-pound bike and a 150-pound rider, and their weight is distributed 50 per cent front and 50 per cent rear at rest. This means the front and rear wheels each carry a 300-pound load. At a normal boulevard stopping pace, the weight transfer amounts to about 75 per cent on the front wheel and 25 per cent on the rear. The front end now weighs three times what the rear does.

At racing speeds the stopping force is greater still. Using the static (or stopped) weight-transfer figures, 90 per cent of the weight or more may transfer to the front, and 10 per cent or less will remain on the rear. The rear end now weighs 60 pounds or less, and the rear brake must stop only 60 pounds of the bike's weight, plus the momentum of the rear wheel and engine.

Rear Brake Overuse

Overusing the rear brake is so common as to be almost a fact of life. **Many riders and racers have given up using the rear brake for hard braking.** It requires too much attention to use correctly, and can cause the rear end to hop or slide when used incorrectly. Both sliding and

Braking forces are awesome. The acceleration of a 150 hp racebike will get it through the 1/4 mile at 145 mph. But the brakes will bring it from 145 mph to 0 in much less distance!

**Weight Transfer
50% Front 50% Rear**

**Weight Transfer
75% Front 25% Rear**

**Weight Transfer
100% Front 0% Rear**

hopping render the bike out of control to some degree. You can't feel good about leaning a bike into a turn if it's basically out of control. You have only two small contact patches on the ground, and when one of them is gone it's a definite disadvantage in traction—one of your main concerns during cornering.

In a panic or race-speed braking maneuver, almost any control will help you more than a locked rear brake. It'd cause you less harm to use the high-beam switch or choke lever. The front is where the weight and stopping power are—not the rear.

The use of the rear brake requires some backwards logic. It seems logical to use the brakes the hardest at the beginning of the braking action, when you're going the fastest. This is true for the front brake. In the back, however, use the lightest rear brake at the beginning of the braking action when the forks are most compressed and the weight transfer is the greatest. As the front brake is released, some of the weight transfers back to the rear wheel and the rear brake can—if it's going to be used at all—do more of the work of stopping or slowing at this time. You have to get smart with your right foot if you want to make any use at all of the rear brake under heavy stopping.

Light Grand Prix bikes or Superbikes have such huge disc brakes and sticky tires that the rear wheel can lift off the ground under heavy braking. Lesser street and race bikes do the same thing, but for a different reason. Hard braking over rippling pavement or bumps can launch the rear end of the bike off the ground because of its unweighted condition. The shocks, which are set to operate under heavier load conditions, contribute to this by not allowing the rear wheel to follow the road. The net result is air between the tire and the road—a very poor traction situation. *Have you experienced this?*

Purpose of Braking

A lot of riders don't pay enough attention to the smooth use of their brakes— even experts.

The purpose of the brakes is to **adjust and correct the speed of the motorcycle downward, controlling deceleration.** You know how sensitive you can be with the throttle; coming out of a turn you can adjust your speed in tenths of a mile per hour by working the twist grip. Going into a turn you can make changes just as accurately with the brakes.

Most riders have the idea that brakes are some kind of on/off switch. Reach a brake marker and pull them on—get down to another marker and let them off. This isn't true. You can't use brakes like that and expect to improve your riding. You're asking too much of yourself. The purpose of brakes is to adjust the speed downward; the overall purpose in racing is to get around the track or down the road quicker, taking seconds off lap times.

One Second Faster

Let's investigate what part brakes play in going one second faster **per lap. On most American tracks you must average about**

one mph faster around the track for a one-second better lap time.
To do this you must go through the turns one mph faster, then hold that advantage down the straights. You won't go faster down the straights if you don't get out of the turns faster. **You have to adjust the speed of your bike accurately to go around the turns one mph faster.** How can you judge that one mph accurately with the bike pitching forward and bouncing over the ripples as you try to compensate for brake fade, and a full tank of gas or an empty one? It's too much to ask. You must treat yourself more kindly and make that one mph easier to find.

Think of the brake as a reverse throttle. Instead of turning the control you pull or press it to start the braking action and downward speed change. **The speed that remains when you release the brakes is the speed you will enter the turn with.** If you want to go one mph faster than the last lap, you must be able to go into the turn that much faster. You can't hope to make up the speed later in the turn—you must set it up right in the beginning. *Where will you try it?*

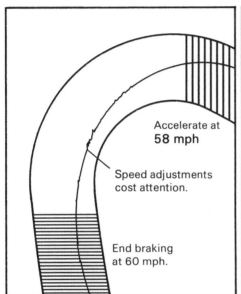

Accelerate at
58 mph

Speed adjustments
cost attention.

End braking
at 60 mph.

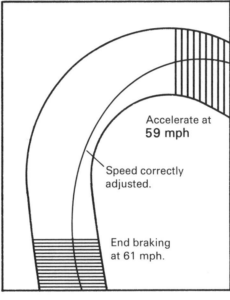

Accelerate at
59 mph

Speed correctly
adjusted.

End braking
at 61 mph.

Late braking often does more harm to lap times and corner speeds than good. Set comfortable brake points for yourself.

Significant Improvements

You can't make significant time improvements by using the brakes harder or going in deeper. You can make time with the brakes by adjusting the cornering speeds accurately.

Where and how you let off the brakes is much more important than where you pull them on, as it sets your cornering speed. You can dive into a 120-mph turn 25 feet deeper than the last time and reduce your lap times about one-tenth of a second. Going in 50 feet deeper would improve it twice as much. If your braking was fine to begin with, you might pick up two-tenths to three-tenths of a second on most tracks. But going in that much deeper just might permanently enlarge your eyeballs, and it would certainly increase the possibility of errors and take up a considerable amount of attention—your ten-dollar bill—that might be better spent elsewhere.

By beginning the braking action at a comfortable location and setting the speed for the turn correctly, you can pick up a second or more every time you use the brakes! By going in too deep and upsetting yourself, you'll only make it more difficult to judge your speed. **It is better to back off on your initial braking marker and allow yourself more time to set your speed right than to panic with late braking.** Resist the temptation to late brake in turns when it won't be an advantage. For passing purposes, you must late brake going into turns. It won't usually improve your lap times, but you can pick up a place in the standings.

Try for your absolute latest braking point in practice so you'll know where you'll wind up on the track if late braking is required in a passing situation during the race.

Look at late braking from the standpoint of time, lap times and your position in the race relative to the other riders. If you're within a second of the fastest rider on the track and can make a lot of improvement in braking, then the two-tenths or three-tenths of a second gained can really do you some good. If you need more than a second to get into winning lap times, don't look for it with the brakes alone; you've got to get your average speed up in turns. *Does it make sense?*

The Product of Braking

The real product of braking is: **To set the speed of the bike correctly for that place on the track so that no further changes are necessary.** If you go in too fast and require more braking when you should be turning, it can throw your timing off. If you go in too slowly and have to increase your speed, that's one extra operation that will take time and effort to correct. **It takes time to realize when something is not right, time to figure out what it should be and time to correct it.** When your speed is set by adjusting it correctly with the brakes, gradually, you won't have to make any corrections and your attention will be free to ride the turn.

Establish a Reference Point (RP) to mark the spot you will begin braking. Braking is a Sub-Product and it involves at least two Points of Timing (POT): one at the point you begin the braking action and one where you have completed it. **It is just as important to establish a marker for the end of the braking as it is to have one for the beginning.** Having a good end-braking marker allows you to see in advance where you'll be finished with the brakes and allows you to adjust your speed more easily. There is no guarantee that the bike will slow down exactly the same amount each lap, even if you brake at the same place—things change. But an **End-of-Braking Marker** will give you a constant to work from. *Will it work for you?*

Braking and Your Sense of Speed

Your sense of speed is your ability to judge whether you are riding faster or slower than you were during previous trips through a turn or section of road. In order to go faster you

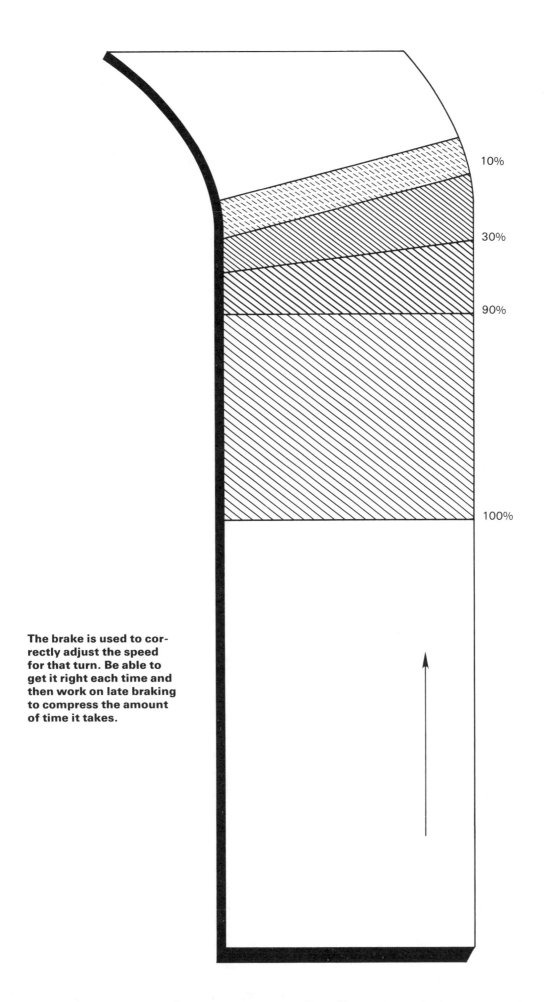

10%

30%

90%

100%

The brake is used to correctly adjust the speed for that turn. Be able to get it right each time and then work on late braking to compress the amount of time it takes.

When my concentration is good I know I did everything right, but it's like I wasn't really there. I get into that frame of concentration and if I go 1/4 mph slower or faster, I know it.

must know what faster is. I calculate that a world-class road racer must be able to judge his speed to within one-half of one mile an hour—and possibly even finer than that. Plus or minus one-half mph gives the rider a one-mph range of sensitivity. A plus or minus sensitivity of five mph allows you up to a 10-mph range in your sense of speed. That might be too much. Five mph faster in a turn is really a great deal—enough to put you down if you do it all at once.

By using the brakes as a dial you can eliminate radical changes in the bike's behavior and make it easier to develop your own sense of speed. Using the brakes as an on/off switch, however, creates dramatic changes in the bike's weight transfer and attitude, which makes the sensing of speed difficult. Using the brakes as a reverse speed dial allows you to reach the speed more gradually and become more sensitive to speed adjustments. The more you are able to sense speed, the easier and quicker it becomes for you to make these speed adjustments accurately.

You can make accurate speed adjustments. There are two results from this:
1. **You develop a better sense of speed.**
2. **You can spend your attention on riding the turn when you get it right the first time.**

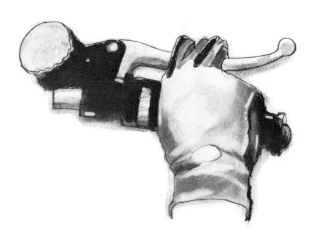

Another Twist to Braking

I let it coast a little in the turn after braking to get everything settled and ready for the exit.

Another twist to braking is that you can effectively increase your speed by letting off the brakes. If you use a comfortable braking point as you enter the turn, then **sense** you may be going too slow, let off the brakes and maintain a speed that will be correct 25 or more feet down the road. If your speed is set right—a little faster than the last lap, you probably won't lose as much time as you might by late braking and upsetting yourself, and leaving the door open for a mistake.

There's a greater advantage to fine-tuning your sense of speed by going into the turns comfortably, without panic, using the brakes as an adjustment, and bringing the cornering speed up a little at a time. Control and confidence can be developed from this skill. *Do you think it will work?*

The Braking Drills

While it is true that you will find the rear brake of little use under hard braking, it's a good idea to find out exactly what happens when it is locked up and sliding. The simplest method is to ride along the track at a comfortable speed, then lock up the rear brake.

Observe one important caution while making this test; if the rear end of the machine slides out of line with the front and you let up on the rear brake, it will—or can—snap back into line with the front wheel. If the front and rear are severely out of line, this action may be so abrupt it could throw you and the motorcycle down.

Some motorcycle safety instructors suggest you can avoid the above situation by leaving the rear brake locked until the machine is stopped, or nearly stopped. This may not always be a practical solution, especially while racing.

It is possible, with practice, to guide the wheels back into alignment with body English and pressure on the handlebars, then let up on the brake and continue. The best situation is to not have locked it up to begin with. Here is a drill you can practice to learn the lock-up point and the sensitivity of your rear brake.

Step 1: Ride along at a comfortable speed in an area with no traffic or distractions.

Step 2: Apply the front brake at a steady and even rate.

Step 3: Apply the rear brake gradually to learn how much pedal pressure it really takes to lock it up.

Step 4: Repeat steps 1 through 3 until you **know** when the brake will lock. Do it at various speeds and braking forces, remembering that the harder you use the front, the lighter the rear will be.

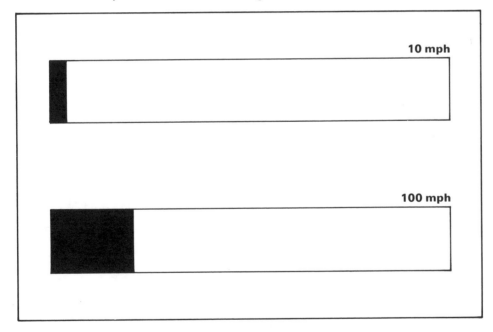

10 mph

100 mph

In straight line braking, a locked-up front wheel feels the same at 100 mph as it does going 10 mph, but the skid mark is longer.

The Front Brake Drill

The purpose of this drill is to find out how much lever pressure is required to lock up the front wheel, and what happens to the bike when the wheel is locked. Without this information you'll always be afraid of the front brake to some degree.

Step 1: Ride along at five to ten mph.

Step 2: Lock up the front wheel, using only the front brake. You will notice that the front wheel turns under or turns in when it is locked, and the bike feels as though it is going to fall over. **It will**—if you keep the brake locked. The simple and only solution is to let off the lever until the slide ends. The bike will straighten up immediately. **The same thing that happens at 10 mph will happen at 100 mph.** The only mistake you can make with a locked front wheel is **not letting off the brake lever soon enough.**

At 100 mph the strip of rubber you put down on the pavement will be longer than the one at 10 mph. If you leave the wheel locked for 1/10th of a second at 10 mph the wheel will slide for 1.5 feet. At 100 mph it will slide for nearly 15 feet. The bike of course has more forces keeping it upright at 100 mph, but it feels the same as it does at 10 mph.

Cutting Costs

The purpose of these exercises is to find the point where the brakes lock, and to become accustomed to that feeling so you'll know what to do if the brakes lock while you're riding. That kind of surprise can cost you $9.00. If you're familiar with it, it costs 25¢ or less.

Step 3: Repeat Steps 1 and 2 above at higher and higher speeds until you are certain what happens, and are certain you can control the machine.

You figure out your brakes, make your decisions on what can be done, and spend that attention on the turn coming up.

Braking and Downshifting

Downshifting is closely associated with braking because the two almost always occur at the same time. From observation, it appears that most riders believe the engine is supposed to help slow or stop the bike. When you hear an engine spinning up toward redline going into a turn, you know the rider is trying to use it as a brake. *Does this apply to you?*

The Engine Is Not A Brake!

It's supposed to increase the speed of the machine—not decrease it. At any place where you have to use the brakes and downshift at the same time, it is not efficient or correct to use the engine to slow you. There isn't much weight on the rear wheel to begin with, and using the engine means you're going to have to replace the crank and pistons sooner. If you wish to slow down the rear wheel a bit, use the rear brake. It's cheaper to replace brake pads than crankshafts. Secondly, it's not correct to use the engine as a brake because that's not the purpose of downshifting. **The purpose of downshifting is to bring the engine**

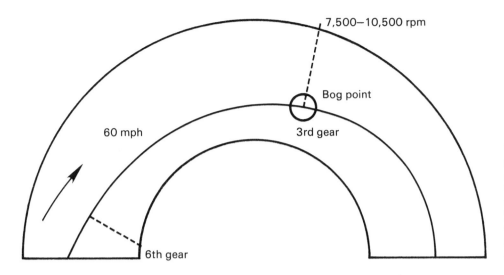

7,500–10,500 rpm

Bog point

60 mph

3rd gear

6th gear

The purpose of down-shifting is to have the engine in the power when you begin to accelerate. You could leave it in sixth gear right up to the point of acceleration and the bike wouldn't care.

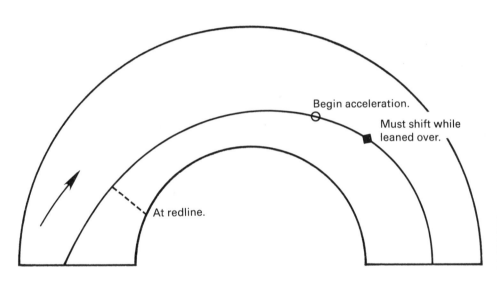

Begin acceleration.

Must shift while leaned over.

At redline.

Up-shifting while still leaned over costs a lot because it must be perfect.

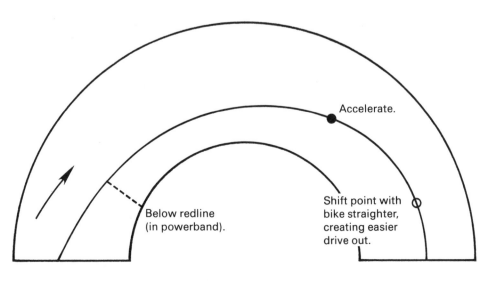

Accelerate.

Below redline (in powerband).

Shift point with bike straighter, creating easier drive out.

With the bike pulling strong off the turn (without up-shifting), you can spend your attention on speed, traction, RPs, etc.

into the right rpm range as you begin to accelerate out of a turn.

Most riders seem to feel it's necessary to downshift as soon as possible after they begin to brake. In some cases there isn't time for a leisurely approach–the downshifting must be done immediately. But if there is time to wait, change gears when you can do it more leisurely.

The Bike Doesn't Care

Going into a turn, the bike doesn't care what gear it's in. The right gear matters only when you begin to accelerate. If you have a third-gear turn at the end of a sixth-gear straight, and part of the turn requires constant-speed running, the bike will not mind if it's in sixth gear through that part of the turn. Of course it's important to make the correct number of downshifts at the proper location. This usually isn't at the first opportunity, just as you begin braking. The best place usually is not when you're in the turn leaned over–that upsets the bike somewhat when the gear changes are made. Changing gears in a turn may cause the bike to bob up and down, as the shifts will affect traction and steering.

The best place to make the gear changes is toward the end of the braking but before the bike is actually put into the turn at a steep lean angle.

You'll save a lot of attention by knowing how many gear changes to make before coming into a turn. If you don't know this, you'll feel you have to start downshifting immediately in case you make a mistake–this is why many riders begin the downshifting too soon. **You don't have to know what gear you're in, so long as you know how many gears you have to go down.** It's amazing how much attention can be freed up by simply knowing this, and doing it. *Should it be tried?*

Tallest Gear Possible

To decide how many gears to go down for a turn, **use the tallest gear possible that still allows the bike to pull the turn in its powerband.** If you go down too many gears and run the turn with the engine spinning up to redline, you are almost guaranteed a gear change while the bike is still leaned over all the way. You will have to make that change in the middle of your drive out of the turn–a place where you need to be concentrating on other things. Sometimes, of course, you might not have a choice with the gearing that is on the bike, and you'll have to change gears while leaned over. Sometimes you can change this situation with the overall gearing so it's correct for the infield turns and overrevs or under revs a little on the straight. If it results in better lap times–and it can–then sacrificing a little top end is worth it. *Any examples?*

Second Problem

The second problem with going down too many gears and red-lining the engine in a turn is that engine vibration can hide the vibration of

In big sweepers I don't let the bike bog down off the power –it seems to slide easier. I keep it spinning up in the power band.

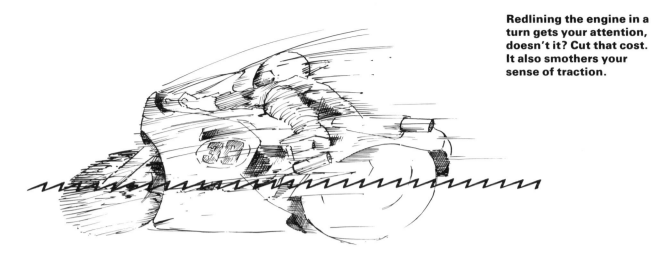

Redlining the engine in a turn gets your attention, doesn't it? Cut that cost. It also smothers your sense of traction.

the tires biting into the road. You need this vibration to tell you your traction situation. There is a vibration when the tires are gripping well and not sliding because they are taking the maximum load. When the tires begin to slide the vibration is different and much finer. **A high-revving engine can, in a turn, cause the rider to believe his tires are sliding.**

Your sense of traction allows you to know what conditions your cornering speeds and lean angles are creating for the tires—how well they are biting into the asphalt. The vibration from this carries up through the frame and you sense it at the handlebars, seat and footpegs. **The changes in that vibration give you a picture of the traction at every moment.** If the engine vibration is "drowning out" or smothering that information, it becomes difficult to sense exactly what the tires are doing. *Are you aware of this?*

Coast Racing

"Canyon racers" have a great pastime called "Coast Racing." Several riders line up at the top of a long hill with lots of turns in it, shut off their engines and begin coasting down. The rider who uses his brakes the least wins. Good riders have noticed they were going faster on the same turns while coasting than when they were riding through them with the engine on. This does not mean you should coast through turns on a race track or anywhere else—you should have the bike in gear so you can control the exit of the turn. This example illustrates that you can "read" tire traction much better when the engine vibration isn't drowning it out. **Note:** I don't recommend Coast Racing because I have seen a number of people get hurt doing it.

I like to use earplugs. The quieter it is the faster I go.

Rider's Job

The rider's job is to be able to **separate the engine vibration from the tire traction vibration so he can constantly sense traction.** Your **sense of traction** is something you **should** be spending

71

a lot of attention on. **The combination of your sense of traction and your sense of speed will help you determine the cornering speed you are willing to use.** No matter what line or RPs or Product you use for a turn, there is a maximum speed for that approach. You won't be able to get that maximum speed if you can't sense the traction of the tires.

You can't ignore the other basics of downshifting: Throttle and clutch action must be correctly timed when changing gears. Downshifting at the right place on the track is important, but failure to rev the engine to match the road speed of the bike will lock up the rear wheel or make it chatter. Always rev the engine to the right speed between downshifts.

Front Brake + Throttle

Most experienced riders have mastered the technique of using the front brake and throttle at the same time. It comes from practice. The purpose of this technique is to allow you to use the front brake as hard as possible and still be able to twist the throttle enough to rev the engine between downshifts. The trick is to be able to keep the brake lever pressure constant, or to change it when necessary while working the throttle.

How you let the clutch out after revving the engine can make a difference between a smooth or a rough gearchange. Good riders let the clutch out smoothly and evenly so the shift has the least affect on the bike. Even if you don't rev the engine enough, letting the clutch out slowly can save the downshift from being rough.

It may seem far-fetched that how and where you downshift can improve your cornering speeds, but I urge you to use the methods in this section to improve your overall riding and sense of traction, as well as to free up more of your attention. *Will this improve your riding?*

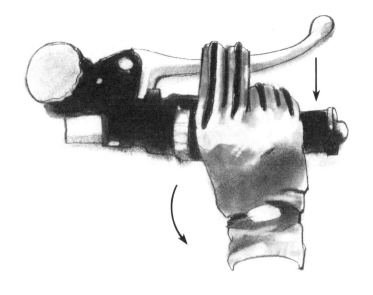

Using the brake and throttle together is an important technique. Performing two things at once cuts costs, whenever possible.

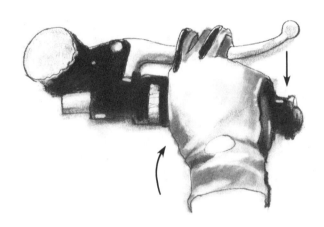

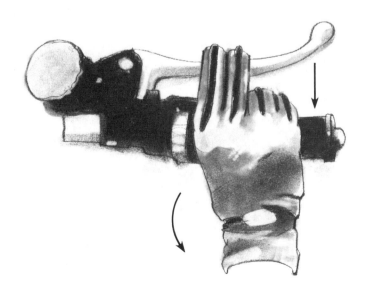

Eddie demonstrates entering the corkscrew, the correct way to end the braking and begin a turn.

1.

Notice the almost unchanged fork extension from beginning to end. That's what is called smooth.

2.

3.

4.

Just as the bike is entering the banked pavement, he begins to accelerate just enough to keep the bike from bobbing up and down.

5.

6.

CHAPTER NINE

Steering

It Happens Backwards

I use countersteering and it just gets right over with very little effort. After I get the bike over then I use the throttle to steer it. I'm drifting both wheels. Let off and it will quit drifting.

Many riders have learned to steer a motorcycle without understanding the process. The purpose of steering is to control the motorcycle's direction of travel. In racing or in any riding situation, you must feel that the steering and the direction of the bike are under your control. The faster you go, the more you want to be certain that the machine will do what you want it to.

Counter Steering

Steering is simple enough—you push the bars in the opposite direction of the direction you wish to travel. That begins the turn, and the bike leans as it turns. Deliberately turning the bars in the opposite direction of travel is known as **counter steering.** Counter means "against," and to steer means to "guide or direct." To go right you must turn the bars left—to go left, turn the bars right. **Counter steering is the only way you can direct a motorcycle to steer accurately.**

This, in fact, is how you've been steering your motorcycle all the time, whether you knew it or not. You cannot steer a motorcycle simply by leaning it. You can get it to veer off in either direction by leaning your weight off to one side at low speeds, but that isn't steering. We are talking about controlling the bike, and that method is something less than control. You can only guess where the bike will go. At speed you can't do much of anything if you're not holding onto the handlebars.

Let's take a look at what happens when you steer. You are approaching a right-hand turn. You lean right, and the bike begins to go right. Since you are holding onto the bars and moving over to the right your left arm is pulling the left side of the bar towards you, which turns the bars to the left. If you lean left to go around a left turn, you pull on the right bar. This must happen if you're holding onto the bars. If you're not holding the bars, the bike will not begin to turn where you lean. You may be pushing on the other bar as well as pulling—it depends on how you hold the bars. *Is it explained?*

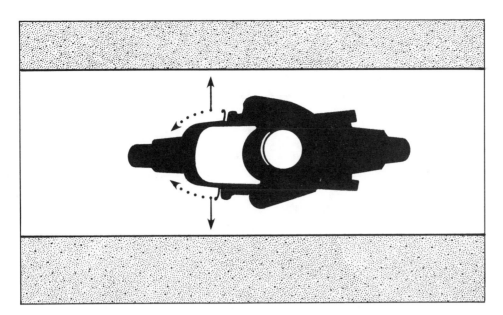

The faster you go, the more precise your steering must be. Products, RPS, Sub-Products, Points of Timing—all become usable with accurate steering.

Push/Pull

As long as you continue pushing or pulling on the bars, the bike will continue to lean over and turn more sharply. When you ease the pressure on the bars, the bike will stay at the lean angle you reached when you eased up the pressure. You don't have to hold the bike into the turn with any great amount of force, if at all. On most bikes, once you have the machine at the desired lean angle, you no longer need to hold onto the bars. Actually, if you were riding 60 mph on most bikes with a cruise control in a huge open parking lot with no bumps, you could take your hands off the bars once you had it leaned over and the bike would continue going around in a circle at that lean angle until it ran out of gas.

When you find yourself holding on very tightly in turns, you're doing a whole lot of unnecessary work. Bumps and other surface irregularities can change the situation of course, so you do have to hold on to make steering corrections. *Do you do this?*

Tighten the Turn

To tighten up a turn and increase your lean angle, you must counter steer again. You're in a right-hand turn, but it's a decreasing-radius and you need to tighten it up. Now you must pull the bars to the left again until you reach the desired lean angle. The same applies in a left-hand turn; you must pull right and lean over more to tighten the turn.

To straighten the bike up after finishing the turn, push the bars into the direction of the turn. Example: You're in a right-hand turn and want to go straight—turn the bars to the right until the bike straightens out.

Riders have problems with this especially on fast, decreasing-radius turns. They get into trouble, then try to force the bars in the direction of the turn. **The major trouble riders have with decreasing-radius turns is in not knowing how to steer.** You can actually see riders climbing onto the tank, exerting a lot of pressure on the bars trying

77

to make the turn. They become rigid as the bike goes further to the outside of the turn and makes them believe they're going too fast. You can see the effort and hear the throttle being rolled off.

Most turns can't be made without correcting for mistakes, camber or radius changes or surface irregularities. Also, to hold a constant radius line through a turn which has changes (camber, bumps, etc.), steering adjustments must be made. Most of your steering occurs with the original steering action going into the turn, but you must be able to correct the bike to compensate for sliding, changes in camber, in radius, or other changes. **If you can't correct the steering in a turn, it will limit you to a "one line through the turn" approach.** Your speed and progress can be limited by how well or poorly you can correct the bike's direction. Any line has a maximum speed that it can be ridden by a particular rider on a particular bike on a particular day. *Any thoughts on this?*

Steering Backwards

In essence, motorcycle steering is backwards from most other forms of transportation. An automobile goes in the direction you turn the wheel, as do most other vehicles. One problem we have in learning to ride stems from a cruel trick played on us by our parents. They gave us a tricycle to pedal around. A tricycle turns in the direction you steer it. When we rode a bicycle for the first time, we fell down, and everyone said it was because we didn't have good balance. Actually, it was because bicycles also counter steer.

Balance had nothing to do with it! The confusion is caused because the child expects the bike to go right when he turns to the right. Eventually, out of sheer survival instincts, he goes through the steering motions without understanding them and winds up on a motorcycle 15 years later not knowing what he has been doing to go around turns.

Practice counter steering and become aware of it. Be aware of how much attention it costs you to start a turn. See if you can remember what happened when you saw an unexpected pot hole or rock on the road and tried to go around it. **Most riders, in an emergency, try to turn the bike in the direction they want to go.** It doesn't work and they find themselves doing some really strange things to make the bike turn. Racing, because of the speed, is a self-created emergency. By thinking and practice, you can lower the amount of time and attention necessary to counter steer down to an acceptable level.

I have known people who have ridden for 30 years without having to face an emergency situation. Then, one day a car pulls out in front of them. They try to avoid it but the bike won't do what they want it to. So they get scared and quit riding. They realize that the control they always thought was there–wasn't. Understanding how a bike steers can help a former rider like this to decide to go riding again.

I have heard varying explanations about what is happening during counter steering, but I have never heard any two engineers agree totally on the physics of it. Despite this, everyone agrees that counter steering is necessary for good control of a motorcycle. Start practicing and applying it to your riding. *Will this improve your riding?*

Kenny Roberts, the master of fast and precise steering, sets up for the right hander in the corkscrew. Notice the wheel sharply counter-steered to the left.

CHAPTER TEN

Slipping and Sliding

Traction: How to Use It and Lose It

Slipping and Sliding Your Way to Victory

Very little winning is done these days without some sliding around on the tires. If you want to win, you'll have to learn to do it, too. **The biggest single breakthrough for most riders occurs when they find out that sliding around doesn't always mean they'll fall. The biggest single drawback is when riders become fascinated with sliding and think it is an end in itself. They must see its purpose.** Sliding is a tool, and that tool should become a useful part of your riding. The first step is the hardest—deciding that it is OK to slide. If you aren't used to sliding, work up to it a little at a time. Don't make a wild decision to run into a turn too fast in hopes you will be able to handle the excess speed by sliding. Work up to it by increasing your speed through the turns until you begin to slide. This usually first occurs when riders get on the gas coming out of slower turns.

Sliding on asphalt can be distracting when over-done, but is a useful riding tool when used in moderation.

Three Kinds of Sliding

Three kinds of sliding commonly occur under racing conditions:

1. The rear wheel begins to spin on acceleration and the rear end "comes around," or goes out more than the front end.

2. The front tire begins "pushing"–it is sliding, but the back is not.

3. Both wheels are sliding, or the bike is in a sideways hop-and-slide motion.

None of these kinds of sliding is caused by braking; they are from going into or through the turn too fast or from using the throttle and breaking traction. *Have you noticed this?*

Exceeding the Limits

Sliding occurs because you have exceeded the limits of tire adhesion for those circumstances. Too much speed or throttle are not the only reasons that sliding can occur–rough pavement or rough riding can also cause it, as can a poor suspension system.

The back end can "come around" all by itself in a turn, which may be regarded as the fourth kind of sliding. Many times this and other kinds of sliding are due to the rider's own handling of the turn, such as when weight transfer to the front or rear causes that end to break away. For example, if you were to come into a turn with just a little too much speed and then roll off the gas suddenly, the front end would become heavier than the rear and could start the front tire sliding. The simple remedy is to crack the gas open slightly to help even the weight on the front and rear. Some bikes are heavier on one end than the other, and have a built-in tendency to slide that end. The road surface can determine which end of the bike slides. Going over a crest, for instance, the lighter end–or both wheels because the downward force is lessened–slides. Usually, however, the wheel with too much weight will break traction first.

Another Decision

Another decision must be made to use the sliding to your advantage. **A good drive coming off a turn usually involves some rear-wheel slippage.** The harder you accelerate, the more rubber you have to accelerate with as the weight transfer generated by the acceleration flattens out the tire and enlarges the contact patch. This holds true only to a point, of course. If the wheel begins spinning too much for effective tire adhesion, it will heat up rapidly and offer very little traction. Allowing it to spin just a bit will allow the bike to continue accelerating and maintain enough traction so it won't slide out completely. You can even steer the bike to your advantage with the rear end slightly loose by pointing the bike to the inside of the turn. This is called "throttle steering."

The next step for the rider who feels he has reached that point

I've only high sided once. I try to keep it sliding and bring it up with the steering, then it quits, especially with a superbike.

where the slide has become a limiting factor in his riding is to use the slide to guide the bike where he wants it to go. As the rider you must decide where and when that slipping around can be used to your advantage rather than just "worrying" the bike around the turn and being limited by the traction. Sliding, you will probably find, costs a fair amount of your $10 worth of attention. **Get used to the sliding and then begin directing the bike with it.**

A moderate and effective slide smoothly done. The slide is obvious because the front wheel is not turned in enough to track at that amount of lean. Note: The slide is being corrected with Kenny's knee. This technique is covered in the following chapter.

Brake Slide

Sliding is a very effective tool to use when you have entered a turn a little too fast. Leaning the bike over a little more just at that point will allow the bike to slide and "scrub off" the extra speed. You don't have to use the brakes and chance something will upset the bike, you simply turn it in a little more, scrub off the extra speed and continue. Traction becomes another matter in fast turns because of the increased amount of attention being spent. Medium speed turns are less of a threat to the rider, he rapidly learns that a little sliding around can work out. Riders tend to be more timid of traction in faster turns. Also, in medium speed banked turns, such as Loudon, sliding is more predictable and less dramatic. The rider can balance off his use of throttle steering against the downward pull of the banking "holding" him in the turn. **Losing traction can sometimes be more of an advantage than keeping it.** *Will it work for you?*

Built-In Safety Valves

Tire sliding and slippage are built-in safety valves. They're telling you the tire is reaching its limits. Premium street tires and racing tires are designed to operate in this area of friction and heat. The used-up rubber "balls up" and goes away, exposing a fresh rubber surface to the pavement. A standard street tire usually will not give up the used and unresilient rubber fast enough, so it's top layers become dry and slippery. The "oils" that are used to keep it resilient have been "cooked" out of that top layer of rubber, but the layer still clings to the tire. If you're not letting your racing tires slip, you're really riding under the ability of the tires.

For your own instructional purpose, I suggest using a tire and rim combination that will allow you to slide the bike around at your level of riding. **Buying racing tires that are beyond your capabilities as a rider will not allow you to experience how tires perform at their limits.** Most new riders can find out more about riding with a set of Dunlop K-81s (which slide very predictably) fitted to their Yamaha TZ250s than they will by mounting a set of state-of-the-art slicks. That goes for other bikes as well. If you are used to riding on sticky tires, but haven't found their limits, mount a set of tires you'll be able to slide around.

The other types of sliding should be approached in the same way. Find out what sliding is like so it won't surprise you when it happens. This will improve your riding, as sliding can cost too much of your attention if you aren't comfortable with it. Once you have sliding under control as just another part of racing, you will be able to use it as a tool. *Will it work?*

You can get away with a lot of sliding on small GP bikes that you can't on a superbike.

CHAPTER ELEVEN

Hanging Off

It Looks Good and It Works

It doesn't look like you're going fast when you are.

Nothing has changed road-racing photography more in the last eight years than the practice and technique of hanging off. Knee dragging is the most dramatic pose racers of any kind have ever indulged in. Spectators are in awe of it, and riders aren't satisfied until they've mastered it. Both canyon and cafe racers are likely to cast in plastic their first pair of designer jeans they touch to the tarmac while hanging off.

Jarno Saarinen was the first rider to exhibit dramatic knee-out riding. He had been an ice racer before coming to road racing, and there knee dragging is both part of the style and the only way to be seriously competitive. Saarinen pioneered it, Kenny Roberts refined it and most everyone who races successfully has picked up knee dragging for himself.

Real Reasons

Aside from the great photography possibilities, there are real reasons for hanging out a body part that is capped by a piece of bone weak enough to be broken by a 40-pound blow. **The first and most useful reason for hanging off is:** you are moving your body weight from the top of the bike to a position that is lower and to the inside. This changes how your weight influences the bike when centrifugal force begins pushing it toward the outside of the turn. When your weight is higher on the bike, it gives the cornering forces a lever to work with. To overcome centrifugal force, the bike must be leaned over in the turn. The greater the force, the more you must lean to overcome it. By hanging off, you move your weight to the inside of the bike and lower to the ground, presenting less of a lever for the forces to act upon. This does not weaken the force, it simply lessens its effect. Now the bike does not have to be leaned over as far to make the same radius of turn, and can go faster without having to increase the lean angle. Even if you go through the turn at the same speed as a rider sitting upright on his machine, you can begin your acceleration sooner than he can because your straight-up bike has more rubber on the road. This can be a tremendous advantage.

Remember, **increasing your speed in a turn effectively decreases the radius of the turn.**

Note: Other suggestions have been made as to why hanging off works. The laws of physics must have something to do with it but my understanding of those physics is limited. Some even argue that it is no real advantage and site rider examples of the past such as Mike Hailwood, who did not hang off. You must try it for yourself and find out if there is an advantage or not.

The leverage theory. A tall mass would tend to have a wider arc than a shorter one, in a turn, at the same speed. Right or wrong, everyone who is currently competitive is hanging off.
Have you ever tried it?

Another Advantage

How much wind resistance does a leg create when it is hung out to the side of a motorcycle at 150 mph? At 100 mph, or even 60 mph? With this additional "sail" on one side, it's easier to turn in that direction. **You can make a quicker and easier steering change with a knee out because the bike and you will pivot around the point of resistance that it offers.**

For the Records

I first noticed this effect of hanging off at Daytona while attempting to set a 24-hour speed record for 750cc machines in 1977. We were riding Kawasaki KZ650 street bikes with large gas tanks and racing tires around and around the outer banked tri-oval at Daytona. Coming off the banking onto the level straights was a steering chore because the centrifugal force was trying to send the bike out to the wall. We were running at a constant speed of about 120 mph. As you might imagine, it was quite boring riding around for hours at a time almost flat out, with the wind tugging at you and trying to lift your helmet off. I still have permanent grooves in my jaw from that chin strap. Out of boredom I began experimenting and found that popping a knee out just as I made a fairly sharp steering change coming off the banks made the steering dramatically easier–by about one-third. The records were set, the champagne was great and I had learned a new tool.

An extended knee offers enough air drag to make steering easier, especially in high speed sections of the track.

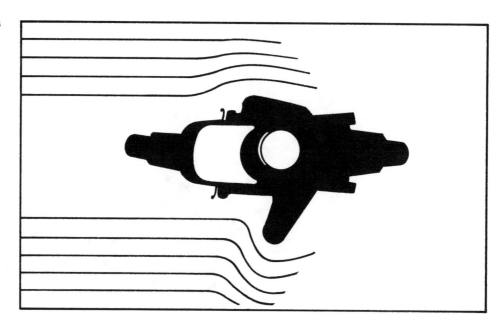

Second Advantage

So, the second advantage of having a knee off is that **steering is easier when the bike and rider pivot around the resistance offered by the extended leg.** Flicking the bike from side to side in esses or any series of turns is much easier when it is timed with the knee coming out just before the steering change is made. This holds true for single turns as well. The liability is obvious–you're creating more wind resistance and the bike will slow down somewhat. Remember, use this technique as a tool; pull it out when you need it and put it away when you don't. This would be especially true with smaller or underpowered machines. Use it only when necessary to make the steering easier.

Third Advantage

A third reason for hanging off has to do with lean angle. Lean angle is one of the indicators you can use to tell how fast you can go and how much traction to expect from the tires. It lets you know where you are in the delicate balance of lean angle, steering, traction and speed. Your knee is a delicate and costly instrument; you must make it your business to know how far it is from the surface of the pavement.

The Knee Gauge

The knee is an incredibly accurate gauge of lean angles–if you put it in the same position each time. To do this your body must be in the

The knee dragging technique is an excellent "curb feeler," or gauge, that is used to determine your lean angle from lap to lap.

same position on the bike each time. Its position can change from turn to turn, but it should be the same each time through a particular turn. Then you can use the distance from the ground to measure: "I was over this far on the first lap and it was OK, so next time around this turn I can go a little faster." The knee doesn't have to drag the whole way around a turn; you can drop it now and then to "sample" your lean angle. *Do you think it will work?*

How You Look and Feel

There are three good reasons to master the skill of hanging off—four if you count the great photo possibilities. Now we get to the fifth reason: **knee dragging gives you a sense of security.** It is strange how this works, and I don't totally understand it, but somehow being in close proximity to the pavement makes falling off seem less dangerous. Perhaps it is because you have already contacted the enemy and know where he is. It doesn't hurt to fall when you're only an inch above the ground. Of course, I'm not taking the speed into account—just the fall.

A fall from the top of the seat is a much longer fall, and that extra distance could be the start of a painful bouncing. Most slide-outs don't result in injury when no bouncing and flipping occur. You judge for yourself whether or not is is any "safer," but it feels more secure.

Sixth Advantage

You may not believe this, but riders have saved themselves from falling because they were able to help the bike back up with their knee after it had begun to slide out. A friend of mine once actually bounced a bike back up onto its wheels with his elbow and continued racing.

You can understand how this might work if you consider the amount of weight that is taken off the bike the moment the knee is on the ground and pushing up. At any rate, this tactic has worked—and will no doubt work again. At an advanced session of the California Superbike School where Eddie Lawson was the guest instructor, he was asked to comment on this. When asked, "How often do you use this technique?", Lawson's reply was "About once a lap." There may be a measure of heroics involved, and certainly five or more layers of duct tape will help keep your leathers and knee looking smart.

Using the knee as an anti-slide device, or an aid to sliding, must also take into account where the slide occurs in a particular turn. A recurring slide becomes a point of timing (POT) in a particular turn. "OK, the bike is going to slide here every time because there is a crest that unloads the bike when I get on the gas." Fine, it's no big deal, you make it part of your plan for that turn. Now, if you keep your knee firmly planted into the asphalt for every turn on every lap of a 20 lap race, you are going to run out of duct tape and start into your knee or leathers. That won't work. What will work is: You get that location on the track really well known, your POT, and you dip the old knee down just before the slide happens. When the slide area is passed, you unweight the knee and save the tape. On the other hand, if you wait for the bike to slide every lap and then put the knee down, it will put you into a minor panic each time it happens. Panics cost a lot.

Here is what you've done to handle the situation.

1. You've found an RP to tell you that the slide area is approaching.

2. You've figured out where to put your knee down. That's your POT.

3. You've figured out where to pick up the knee, at the end of the slide area. That's another POT.

4. You've turned the drifting or sliding into a predictable part of the turn.

5. You've saved many dollars worth of attention that can be

The knee is extended in readiness to correct for sliding, should it occur.

used for judging speed, adjusting your line, passing, throttle control, figuring out a better plan, getting a better drive, etc., etc. *Can it be done?*

Hang Loose

Never become rigid while hanging off. Be relaxed and settle into the position you normally take while in this maneuver. You've got to be as relaxed as possible so that you don't become a bobbing weight on the bike that acts like a passenger who doesn't know how to relax. If you encounter any kind of rough pavement or handle the bike roughly, it will move up and down. If you're loose, you will flex up and down with it. If you're rigid, the bike will go into its motion, then you will, then the bike will move again, creating a wobble.

Be comfortable rather than stylish.

Don't use the handlebars to support your weight when you hang off. This sends inputs to the steering and can start a wobble as well. Use your legs to get from one side of the bike to the other, and hold on with your outside leg. Then relax.

I'll see you in the photos.

Note: Many riders have found that a little talcum powder on the seat is helpful when changing from side to side. *Will it work for you?*

Note:

If you don't feel comfortable hanging off, don't do it. You can waste a lot of time and effort trying to work out something you don't need to do. Use hanging off as a tool. When you begin to have ground clearance problems while cornering, or any other problems that could be helped by hanging off, then do it.

A rider's style includes how well he accomplishes each of the parts of riding. It is all of what he understands and all of what he doesn't feel good about rolled into his own package. Hanging off may be part of your riding package, or it may not be, right now.

A rider tells a great deal about himself by his style. For example, a rider who can stay tucked down behind the bubble and low on the bike in fast or tricky sections knows the track. He has RPs, Points of Timing and other factors well understood. The rider who doesn't will be sitting up trying to see where he is going.

Don't hang off if you don't need to.

Style is based on where the rider is spending his $10 worth of attention. Fitting yourself into a style for no reason can cost you a lot.

CHAPTER TWELVE

Passing

Who Was That I Just Passed?

It is sometimes easier to pass a rider you are racing with, someone with equal or similar ability to your own, than it is to pass lapped or slower riders. The other racer on your level is there long enough for you to make out some aspect of his riding style, where the slower rider is a new and unobserved commodity. Many times you will become wary of these riders just from the fact that they are a lap down on you. It makes you wonder if they know what's going on.

Passing comes up often in new-rider discussions. It is definitely one of the crafts involved in racing and something that only a few, even of the top riders, have mastered.

The ground rules in passing and following will increase your understanding of the actions involved:

Ground Rules of Passing

1. **Motorcycles go to the outside of the track when they fall, and so do riders.** If you are directly behind a rider and he loses control and falls, it is almost impossible to hit him. **By the time you get to the place he fell he will no longer be there.** Aluminum side covers and fairings offer little traction, so once the bike is over, it will rapidly travel to the outside.

If you're positioned to the inside of another rider and he falls, it is not possible to hit him. The only exception to this is in high, banked turns such as at Daytona. There the banking is so steep that the sliding machine and rider will travel fairly straight for some distance, then begin a downward course to the inside of the turn. Bike and rider literally fall down the hill because the cornering force is no longer holding them up on the banking. Lesser banked turns have a similar but somewhat less dramatic tendency to do the same thing.

Passing on the outside has increased liabilities because this maneuver makes it possible to intersect the path of a fallen rider or machine on its outward swing.

2. **Often, two-rider accidents are the result of the trailing rider following the lead rider, the first to fall, off the track.** One of the concrete examples of the old axiom, "You go where you look."

It is very upsetting to have someone fall off in front of you and it can possibly be dangerous to you. All too often, the trailing rider will watch the fallen one and go down with him. Perhaps it is because the fallen rider is now having a more interesting ride, perhaps it is the danger. It may be just morbid curiosity. Whatever the reason, the simple solution is to not look at the fallen rider. Continue going where you had originally intended and there is little possibility of becoming entangled with him.

3. **If you become involved with watching the rider in front of you, passing becomes very difficult.** Spend your attention on that rider and you are not spending it on where you are going–your $10 bill has not expanded.

Guys get in trouble watching the rider in front. You're aware that they're there, but you look at the track.

Also, if you are looking at another rider you are using him for a RP and not looking at the RPs that you know will get you through the turn. You become lost.

Here's some advice, and an example, of riding in traffic from three American masters: Kenny Roberts, Eddie Lawson and Mike Baldwin. I have seen each of them run near-perfect laps, only tenths of a second slower than their best race laps, in very heavy traffic.

Baldwin says he treats slower riders like trees in the woods. He considers them stationary objects he is going by.

Lawson suggests the correct procedure is in not looking at the leading rider.

After Kenny Roberts' incredible opening lap at Sears Point, where he went from 32nd to sixth on a track that doesn't really have a straightaway, nobody even bothered to ask him. He obviously didn't consider there was anyone else there.

Look where you want to go, not at the rider you are about to pass. The attention spent on him is the amount you need to get by.

4. Following other riders can help you learn the track layout when it isn't clear to you. Following too close can be a liability, but following at a comfortable distance can improve your own mastery of a turn. When a rider is out in front of you he creates a "rolling RP."

Let's say another rider is ahead of you by 25 to 100 feet. If the track surface is hard to see because of elevation changes or radius changes you can know where the track is going by locating the other rider. So long as he stays on the track, his presence lets you know there is asphalt ahead of you. It gives you a better picture of what you can't see. As you draw closer you must then abandon him as an RP, keeping your attention on your Product, Sub-Product or RPs. *Does it make sense?*

Passing Signals

In California it is legal to split lanes—to ride between the lines of cars on the freeway. From this practice, California riders have learned that the auto driver always does something before he changes lanes. It may be a look in the mirror, a twitch of the head, shoulder movement, a glance to the rear or a change of hand position on the steering wheel. In racing, a rider often makes a movement, usually of the head, just before changing directions. It isn't always true and it isn't 100 per cent effective as it seems to be with car drivers, but it does happen and you can use it if you see it.

Your ability to "read" the other rider's line and where it will put him has a lot to do with passing. A rider who is leaned over the the maximum limits of his machine is not likely to make any radical moves toward the inside of the track. His line of travel is pretty well set. You must be able to size up his line, determine where it will take him, and decide if you can make the pass.

Judging the amount of space that you need for a pass isn't all that difficult. **It only takes a little more space than the width of a doorway to pass another rider.** If you can see that amount of space, you can get through. *Will this help?*

Basics Apply

In passing, the basics of riding still apply. You must spend your attention on getting around the track, not on other riders. Your RPs, Sub-Products, Products, what you do, timing and the ability to concentrate on the track will be the deciding factors in who crosses the finish line first.

The width of a common
doorway is all the track
that is necessary to pass.

This sequence represents two seconds of time. A well-executed pass from the set-up through to completion.

1.

2.

3.

4.

5.

6.

CHAPTER THIRTEEN

Supervise Yourself

Yes, Homework **Is** Necessary

*I go into a race, on the start-
ing line, with the attitude that
I'm gonna get beat—these
guys are gonna smoke me.*

To help supervise your racing program, keep accurate records and be working on some aspect of it each time you go to the track. This way, you'll be making the best use of your time, expensive track time and of your bike.

Record Your Lap Times

The first absolutely necessary record to keep is of lap times. **Lap times indicate your overall base-line improvement from lap to lap and race to race.** Lap times tell you directly what your efforts are bringing in terms of improvement. When you try something new, the lap times are a sure-fire way of weeding out what is working from what is not.

Keeping accurate records is nothing more than keeping a diary of your riding. Decide what you are going to work on and make a note of it in the book. **Go to the track with a plan.** That plan should include all of the information you have gathered there on previous laps. If you haven't ridden the track before, start from the beginning, learning the course and all its peculiarities. You might also start at the beginning of this book and go through the track, working on the points mentioned in each chapter. Notice the construction of the track itself, what **products** you are likely to have for each turn or section of the track, note what you are doing in each, what **reference points** you're using, or have available to use, how your timing is working in each section, what decisions you're operating on, where the barriers are and what to do about them. See what you can do to slick up your braking and shifting, or how more conscious steering could make your way around the course easier. *Do you agree?*

Improve Problem Areas

Pick up your problem areas and try to better them; leave your strong points alone for now. A good way to check your progress on the track will require two good stopwatches and a person to act as timer. This will help you narrow down the areas you're working on so that you can see if you're gaining or losing time in a particular section. The timer should be in a position to see the whole track, or at least most of it. The stop watches should be the variety that can record every lap, or you may use two or three single lap timers.

Break the Track

Break the track into sections and time each one separately. You might have your timer clock from, for example, the start/finish line to Turn Three; Turn Three to Turn Six, then Turn Six to the start/finish line. The timer will record your times for each section, then record the overall lap time beside it. Now you'll know exactly <u>where</u> you need work. I have seen, for example, Wayne Rainey—formerly a Class C dirt tracker—run a box-stock Kawasaki KZ750 through a tight section at Willow Springs Raceway (from Turn Three through Turn Six) faster than nationally-ranked riders on their Superbikes! Rainey's bike was equipped with street Dunlops, and the Superbikes ran slicks on wide rims plus they had considerably more ground clearance.

If you can also time your competition, you may find where they are picking up time on you and where you need to get your times down. Your only limit is the number of watches you have and the people you have to run them. This is valuable, bottom-line information you can work and think with. *Should it be tried?*

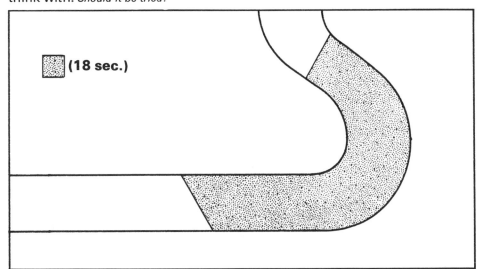

(18 sec.)

Breaking the track into three or more timed sections pinpoints your improvement.

Work On One Thing At A Time

When you supervise yourself, go out intending to improve one turn or one aspect of all the turns, like braking, reference points or points of timing. When you do this, don't change anything else. Keep the rest of the track and what you're doing there the same. This will give you a better picture of the results.

You can think of endless things to do while you're out on the track, but stick to your plan and just work on what you had intended to from the start.

I like the big sweepers, fast corners. Sometimes the guys I'm lapping go through the slow ones faster than me.

You can also try to do nothing. Homework isn't fun all the time, so take a few laps when you can and just ride. Don't concentrate on any improvements. At the most, try to relax more and concentrate on your breathing. Often, I have seen great forward surges in lap times by riders who were instructed to just take a few laps for fun. This is the time when you can integrate all the things you were working on into a smooth and flowing ride. You go out and ride just like you know what you're doing.

Go Faster

Freddie (Spencer) *is fearless coming out of slow turns.*

Most riders try to go faster each time on the track. That is a whole decision in itself that should be reserved for racing and for when you have done a good amount of thinking about the track. Once you've gone through the boring parts of looking and experimenting to see what works, you are armed with enough knowledge to make your decision to go faster really work. **Without solving some of your barriers and rough spots on the track, you just make mistakes at a higher speed.** It has been said many times by many good riders: **First do it right, <u>then</u> add the speed. "Right"** is what works best for you and produces the best lap times. Set your plan then add the speed. That's your starting place. *Can you apply this?*

Use practice to your best advantage. If you're one of the fastest riders that day, go out in front of the practice session so you won't have to cut through a lot of traffic. If you're one of the slower riders, go out towards the end of the group and stay out of the distracting traffic.

Practice = Information = Think

Come back from each practice session with information you can use to think with. Whether you are working on some aspect of your racing or just taking a relaxed ride, have a solid idea of what went on during the laps you have just run. **If you have a hard time remembering what you have just done, your attention is so stuck on something that you don't have enough of it left to observe yourself.** This happens more than we like, and it makes it difficult to operate with understanding. When you can't remember, your precious ten-dollar's worth of attention is being spent to such a degree on something else that you only have time to operate. This will leave you short on understanding and makes it difficult to tell what works and what doesn't.

Waste Paper, Not Track Time

Paper is cheap—use it to make drawings of the turns and to show yourself what you're doing in them—make X's and O's on the drawings to indicate the RPs, POT, Products and your plan of attack to get around the course faster. Draw one turn at a time unless you have some esses.

Make your own drawings–don't use track diagrams. **What counts is how the turn looks to you.** Track diagrams are fine for helping spectators find their way to the grandstands, but they don't include camber changes, rough spots, exact locations of uphills and downhills, etc.

Track Drawings

Make your track drawings as exact as possible. Anyone who can ride a motorcycle can make a simple line drawing of a turn. It doesn't take artistic ability. If you find it difficult to make a turn drawing after you've ridden the track, sleeping through art class wasn't the problem, **you just don't know the turn.** Parts of it are still unclear to you. **A drawing makes your thoughts one step closer to the real thing.** Paper isn't asphalt, but it is closer to it than the stuff that thoughts are made of. Drawings get you involved in a very direct way with what is going on while you're riding.

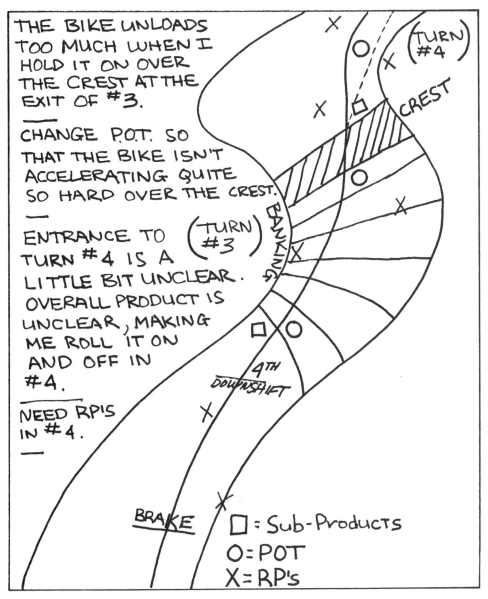

THE BIKE UNLOADS TOO MUCH WHEN I HOLD IT ON OVER THE CREST AT THE EXIT OF #3.

CHANGE P.O.T. SO THAT THE BIKE ISN'T ACCELERATING QUITE SO HARD OVER THE CREST.

ENTRANCE TO TURN #4 IS A LITTLE BIT UNCLEAR. OVERALL PRODUCT IS UNCLEAR, MAKING ME ROLL IT ON AND OFF IN #4.

NEED RP'S IN #4.

(TURN #4)

CREST

(TURN #3)

BANKING

4TH DOWNSHIFT

BRAKE

☐ = Sub-Products
O = POT
X = RP's

Drawings bring your thoughts one step closer to the track. Work out problem turns on paper.

Have you ever tried it?

Fast = Fast

You gain more time in the fast turns than you do in slow ones. You will find, as every rider has, that a little faster in the fast turns makes much more difference than a little faster in the slow ones. You cover more distance in the fast turns, which brings up your overall average faster. Remember, it takes only about one mph higher average to go one second faster per lap. A typical slow turn may be 100-150 feet in length, while a fast one may be 300 to 900 feet or more. That is a larger part of the track in which your average can be higher.

Racer's Tools

(1) Look at your riding from the standpoint that you intend to improve. (2) Set yourself lap-time targets for the day. (3) Make sure you come off the track with information you can use. (4) Make every practice session count even more by working on a particular point while you're riding. (5) Don't become discouraged. (6) Read over the material in this book again after you have ridden. It will make more sense to you then.

Can you see it working for you?

GOING DOWN THE FRONT STRAIGHT INTO TURN ONE, I RAISE UP AND SHUT OFF THE THROTTLE JUST BEFORE THE RED CONE. THEN I DOWN SHIFT ONE GEAR, THEN START MOVING MY REAR OVER TOWARDS THE LEFT AND LEAN LEFT. THEN I START ROLLING THE THROTTLE BACK ON IN THE CENTER OF THE CORNER, STILL LEANING LEFT AND GRADUALLY RAISING THE BIKE UP STRAIGHT. THEN DOWN THE SHORT SHUTE INTO TURN TWO. AS I APPROACH TURN TWO I START TO LEAN RIGHT ABOUT FIVE FEET FROM THE OUTSIDE EDGE OF THE TRACK, ROLLING THE THROTTLE 1/2 OFF, LEANING RIGHT AND GOING THRU THE CENTER OF THE TURN ABOUT 3/4 THROTTLE. AS THE TURN STARTS TO TIGHTEN UP, I ROLL THE THROTTLE ON LEANING THE BIKE TOWARDS THE INSIDE POLE. THEN I AM GOING STRAIGHT. TURN THREE IS APPROACHING. I SHUT OFF THE THROTTLE, DOWNSHIFT ONE GEAR AT THE RED CONE AND APPLY THE FRONT AND REAR BRAKES, LEAN LEFT AND ROLL THE THROTTLE BACK ON AS THE TURN LOSES IT'S BANKING. BY THEN I'M STRAIGHT AND LEANING RIGHT INTO TURN FOUR. I AM ON THE INSIDE POLE AS I ENTER THE TURN, ROLLING THE GAS BACK ON, I AM ABOUT FIVE FEET FROM THE OUTSIDE EDGE OF THE CENTER OF THE CORNER. AND THEN I AM LEANING IT OVER HARD FOR THE EXIT OF THE TURN.

CHAPTER FOURTEEN

Advice

Ask Your Best Friend: You

One word of advice about people giving you advice about your riding–**you are your best advisor.** You're the one sitting in the saddle and riding. No one has better information about what is going on in your head than you. Deal with **y<u>our</u> own decisions, y<u>our</u> barriers, y<u>our</u> products and reference points, y<u>our</u> points of timing and attention**–not someone else's.

I'm not one for giving out advice. I don't want to give it away, especially at the track or race day when someone has a particular question. But I won't screw a guy up and give him wrong or dangerous advice.

Sort It Out for Yourself

The way your riding looks to someone beside the track has nothing to do with how you are thinking about it. In the end you have to sort it out for yourself. Another rider's line, even if he goes faster than you, might not be the correct one for you. Information can be valuable, but you have to watch where it's coming from and who's giving it. Other riders are often operating from their own false information. Pick it up and you will try to make it work, too. It can waste your time and energy.

I have tried not to give you advice about riding in this material–instead, I've tried to explain what happens while you're on a motorcycle, and what a rider must think of when speed and precision are important. It's your job to decide how they apply to you. *How do you feel about it?*

You are the one who has to ride the track. A nickel's worth of bad advice could cost a lot more ($10) on the track.

Behind the race face, the glare of concentration. Pumping up the adrenalin or going over his plan?

CHAPTER FIFTEEN

How to Fall

Relax—You're Just Road-Testing Your Leathers

Three really important factors about falling off a motorcycle are: What you do when the time comes to unload—How you keep this bad situation from getting worse—and How you feel about the business of falling off.

Be Willing to Fall Off

Let's consider the third factor first. As a racer, you should be <u>willing</u> to fall off. You don't have to <u>want</u> to, but being willing to is very different, and it has to do with your attitude about falling. If you ride a motorcycle—and especially if you race one—falling is an activity you're likely to become involved with. It goes with the territory of riding. **If you resist falling, you are more likely to fall.** This is the key—it works very similarly to a target fixation. That's where you look at an object you don't want to hit, then become so fixated on the threat that you don't look for a way out and hit it anyway. Falling is similar in that the more you resist it—or fixate on the idea of <u>not</u> falling—the more it will take your attention away from your riding. You can spend your entire ten-dollar's worth of attention resisting falling, then because you have no attention left to operate the machine, fall from a mistake.

Here again is the magic of the **decision.** You simply decide that you might fall off and accept that it <u>can</u> happen, at any time, anywhere. You have to look at it and say, "Okay, I <u>can</u> fall off one of these things. I might break a bone or have a hell of a slide, or I just might die doing it." All of these things <u>can</u> and do happen to motorcycle riders. So, get it out of the way by taking a look at it and then making your decision from there. I wouldn't advise racing to anyone who wasn't willing to fall down.

Falling Insurance

No one <u>wants</u> to fall down, but once you've done it and it comes out alright, falling isn't as fearsome any more. **Your best insurance against falling is to not resist it.**

If you <u>do</u> fall, however, here's how to come out of it with the least amount of damage to your body:

Let Go

1. **Let go of the bike:** It is much larger and heavier than you and very likely to travel further down the road than you will. If you're holding onto it, you're going along for the ride. You want to minimize your motion so your new leathers don't get holes ground through them. Motorcycles have hard things sticking out their sides that can catch on the ground and send them rolling and doing endos. If you're still attached to the bike, you'll do the same. When you let go, the difference between your weight and the bike's will generally drop you off at some other place.

2. **Relax:** If you lose it, just relax. Don't do anything. The act of relaxing will usually get you away from the bike. If you extend your arms or legs to try to break your fall, you will be providing yourself with a pivot that can send you flying or tumbling. When your body's rigid it's easier to break things. If you're relaxed, skidding along like a rag doll, it's more difficult to break bones.

In a fall, let go. Motorcycles are out of your control once they begin to slide on the sidecovers. Holding on will extend your trip.

Relaxing completely will spread out any impact and help protect against broken bones. Scuff up a lot of the leathers a little bit, not scuff a little part a lot.

Relaxing also puts more surface area onto the ground and spreads the impact over a larger area. For example, if you weigh 150 pounds and fall on your palm, that three square inches of your palm will take a force of about 50 pounds per square inch from the fall alone–the force of that impact will increase greatly with the speed. If you land on your back, arms and legs instead, you're falling onto a couple square feet which brings the load per square inch down below one pound. A pound dropped on your hand will hurt a little bit. Fifty pounds dropped on your hand will hurt like hell.

Relaxing spreads the impact over a larger area. This is one of the techniques used by stunt men and martial arts people to lessen the possibilities of pain and damage to their bodies.

Probably everyone has heard of exceptional situations where the rider slides out, then climbs on top of the bike and waits for it to stop. He never touches the ground and is unhurt. You decide if you want to try this, but understand that the worst kind of fall is when the bike is sliding along and something catches which flips it over on the other side. If you're still hanging on–you get launched. This is called "high-siding" when you're thrown over the high side of a bike in a turn. "Low-siding" is when the bike is leaning over and the tires wash out, dropping it straight down.

Stop Before Standing

One other important aspect of falling is that sometimes you can't tell when you've stopped. Strange as this may seem, it's true. When you fall, it upsets the inner-ear fluid that governs your sense of balance and motion. **You can think you are actually stopped while still sliding along at 100 mph.** It can make for an exciting time if you decide to stand up before the sliding has stopped. It has happened to me and I've seen it happen to other riders. You wind up taking 15-foot strides down the track, and you look like a kangaroo. To avoid this, count to three when you think you have stopped, then look around to see if the sky and ground are where they're supposed to be. *Some examples?*

Practice Falls

As I mentioned, you prepare for the possibility of falling by relaxing. Here's an exercise to help you do that:

1. Stand up in the middle of a carpeted room, or use a gym that's equipped with wrestling mats.

2. Extend both your arms to the sides to shoulder height.

3. Command them to relax and just let them fall. If you notice any resistance in your muscles after you have made the command, do it over until your arms just flop down to your sides.

4. Stand in the middle of the room and command your whole body to relax. Just let go of it and let it fall. If you do it honestly your legs will buckle first and you won't fall straight forward or straight backwards– you'll crumple to a heap on the floor. Do it until you can completely relax

your body on command.

If you want to be creative with this drill you can do it on soft mats while walking or running. You can also do it on a trampoline. The important thing is to relax the body on command so it will fall relaxed and spread the impact over a large area. I have road-tested this technique at over 130 mph and can personally testify that for most motorcycle accidents you'll have a much better chance of avoiding injury if you hit the ground relaxed. *Do you agree?*

After A Fall

If you try to dodge oncoming traffic, there is a greater chance you'll be hit. Look at it from the point of view of the other riders— they have a chance to avoid you if you stay in one spot. If you're up and moving in a panic, they don't know which way you'll run. If you're stopped, they have something to avoid. Also, it's much better to have a leg run over by another motorcycle than to be hit by one while you're standing up.

A plan of action, such as relaxing when you fall off, is like wearing a helmet. You don't need it until you hit the road, then you <u>really</u> need it. Being willing to fall off will help keep you off the ground; knowing how to do it can minimize your injuries.

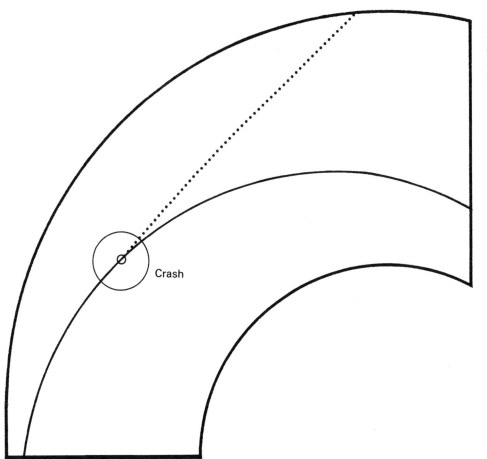

Crash

A motorcycle and rider will widen their arc of travel after a crash, except in heavily banked turns.

CHAPTER SIXTEEN

Sponsorship

There Is No Free Lunch

I'll get to the nitty of sponsorship right away: you need one of three things—or all three—to get sponsorship support.
1. Know someone who is in a position to sponsor you.
2. Work hard promoting yourself and cover every possible sponsor.
3. Be so good at racing that other people want you on their team carrying their stickers and leathers.

A P.R. World

In most cases, people want to sponsor riders they like. Sometimes, that's more important than your ability to ride, but usually it just helps a lot. Your potential sponsor may picture you on the winner's stand at Daytona saying great things about him. He may just picture you at the club races saying good things about his product to others. Are you the kind of person that others believe? Your sponsor—or potential sponsor—must understand one thing if he is to be at all successful. **We live in a P.R. (public relations) world and good P.R. helps.** If you just expect to be a club racer and nothing further, this doesn't exclude you from the fruits of sponsorship. Local racing has been the spawning ground for some of the most successful product lines ever. *Have you noticed this?*

His Honor, The Racer

Racers are opinion leaders in their fields. That field is motorcycling. Throughout racing history, the majority of products that are sport- or performance-related have shown up on the race track, then on many street bikes.

If you have raced and have friends, you will notice that your credibility has increased among them. Your friends and their friends are depending on you to give them the hot tip on performance parts and even on what bike to buy. An opinion leader is somewhat of a celebrity. You, as a racer, must fulfill the requirements of a celebrity. If you have any success in racing, be willing to answer endless questions about motorcycles. Your sponsor should understand that you are willing to promote his products. When you are a great racer, nobody will expect you to do any of this because you will have become overpaid and cocky. Not really—but the winning will be first priority.

The basis for sponsorship, whether you are a good racer or not, is the exchange you can make with the sponsor. What can you do for him and what is he going to do for you?

Step One is getting the sponsor. Step Two is spreading his name around. Step Three is win, win, win.

Decide, Plan and Do!

It's up to you to decide upon and sell to your potential sponsors the exact plan you have for getting his name out into the world in the best possible light. Plan for activities such as arranging for articles, making your pit area into a sort of mini trade show for his products, showing him that you have a sphere of influence, pointing out that racing is—and has been—good promotion, and anything else you can dream up to show him how it will benefit him. Then do it!

Keep your sponsor informed of what you're doing, or propose that you will inform him. Take pictures, write letters and keep him up to date. *Can you do it?*

Proposals

Proposals should be well-organized and look professional. If you outline a great season of promotion and show up with a dirty or disorganized proposal, he will see through it from the start. He won't be confident that you are the conscientious, well-organized person he needs to do the job. You must begin to think of yourself as an employee of a company in which you own shares of stock.

Don't promise anything you can't deliver. Think out the year

109

ahead and write up a plan you can actually carry out. The number of companies that will pay you to run stickers at the amateur level is dwindling and has almost disappeared. Don't base a sponsorship package on the fact you will run his stickers on your bike. Too many riders will run stickers for a quart of oil or just for fun. Design your package so it will stand on its own whether you have stickers on the bike or not. Propose to make yourself available for promotional activities. *Any thoughts on this?*

The Year Ahead

The most important part of any sponsorship package is one that you and your sponsor must both be well aware of. I have seen it overlooked countless times with unfortunate results. At the beginning of the year companies are looking around to see how they will spend their promotion dollars. They are enthusiastic and expect that the coming year will be good. They have dollars that they feel compelled to spend. The advertising people are pumping them up for the coming season. It is winter and the grass will be greener in the spring. You go in with a good proposal and everything looks right. You're pumped, the company is going to give you $500 and all the product you can use. It will be a help.

The season begins and you go about promoting the product as you said you would. When the season ends, you go back to your sponsor to see about next year and he says, "What did you do for me this year?" You talked up the product and spent a lot of time keeping up your commitment, but now it all slips away from you and it seems petty to mention each time you talked to a group of riders on the Sunday ride to pump his product, each time you carefully placed stickers on the john walls, every time you got someone to believe you about it.

Here's the Deal

If the sponsor spends money on you, he had better be willing to spend more money telling people about it. Sponsorship is a two-way street. You don't get something for nothing and neither does he. It takes an effort on both of your parts to get the word out. On the club level he should be supplying you with banners and pins and stickers to give away, and maybe an ad in Cycle News to commemorate your good performance. A race program ad, for instance, helps him get his name out and also makes you better known at the same time. The sponsor builds his rider and his product at the same time. It's a P.R. world, and the more they see of you and the product, the better P.R. it is. You've got to have your sponsor agree to back you throughout the year—win, lose or draw.

If the sponsor won't back you in this way, find another sponsor. Your guy doesn't understand what he is sponsoring you for in the first place, and you will lose him when he loses his initial enthusiasm. At the end of the year, if he has used his resources to put you and his product out there, he won't ask you what you did for him—he will <u>know</u>. As riders, we have to eliminate this idea that there is some kind of magic that goes along with racing. A win—or lots of wins—will not do anything for the sponsor. It will be his follow-up that gets the word out. *Do you get it?*

Your P.R. Program

Even without a bunch of first places you can still do plenty to make yourself known. Racing is still such an unknown quantity—in the U.S. especially—that you can promote yourself on late-night radio talk shows, public-access TV and taking part in civic-minded activities during the off-season such as talking to boys' clubs. Start a "Get racing off the streets and onto the track" program that might save a life or make a racer of someone. You can even plug your sponsor here. Local newspapers are always hungry to fill space with stories about local people. You can go into one of them with the same civic-minded approach and it would be difficult for them to turn you down. Urge other riders to do the same. It may seem you're sharing the spotlight, but in the end it makes racing more popular, which gives sponsors a better reason to participate. *Any examples?*

Satellite Sponsorship

Your key target is one well-known sponsor. This allows your other sponsors something to identify with, something larger to be connected with than just Joe Smith, racer. They revolve around and bask in the light of the better-known central sponsoring company. The possible advantages of being a satellite linked to a large company with a multi-million-dollar advertising budget is very appealing to the smaller business-man. You are doing him a favor by linking him with your central sponsor.

For example, when a new man is signed onto a factory team, in many cases he is still an unproven rider—high potential obviously, but he has not yet won any races. Still, a new team rider for any factory has little difficulty in finding sponsors that will pay handsomely for a patch on the leathers. The sponsor is now connected to the factory team and the factory advertising campaigns. The rider, in this case, is of secondary importance. The sponsor may pay the rider $5,000 for placing the patch or stickers, but the factory may use photos in millions of dollars worth of ads, posters and promotional items. *Some examples?*

Big Fish

Landing a big sponsor can be useful in helping you gather satellite sponsors. Going to a big company with a small, but effective plan that will not drain the promotional budget can be of more value to you than is going in with an expensive program that may be turned down. It is still the same idea as above. Large companies like to get bargains, too, and the smaller company feels connected. Remember, your contract terms may be kept confidential if you choose so the other sponsors you approach don't know whether you are getting $10,000 or $100. Keep it that way.

Where To Fish

The size of the pond you fish in for sponsors is important. A factory is a large fish in a large pond, worldwide. They have the money to buy the best. If you are not the best–yet–start fishing in a smaller pond to begin with. You may only get a set of shocks from your local accessory store, but that now makes you appear connected to something larger. You are a satellite and revolve around your sponsor as well. If you can do a great job of promoting the shocks there might be some gas money the next time you talk to the sponsor. Plaster their name over everything you can, and even spend money on your own to prime the pump. (It makes you look like you're getting more from your sponsor, and a new sponsor will expect to pay more from what he has seen in the past.) Move up the sponsor ladder one size pond at a time. You may even start in a large puddle, but at least it is wet. *Does this apply to you?*

Over the Limit

Once you begin to catch sponsors, don't go over the limit–throw back the small ones. If you come out on race day with 30 stickers on your bike and leathers, your sponsor may have to ask where his name is. Pick the best sponsor and make him the central figure, then don't crowd your space. A few sponsors, three to five, still allow everyone to get his share of exposure without feeling lost. Think of your own time also. You won't be able to do as good a job promoting 10 products as you will with only three.

That's Show Biz

Sponsorship is the business end of the racing game. It has little or nothing to do with the riding itself except for one very important thing: **having enough money to operate your program buys you time to concentrate on yourself as a rider.** Spending all your time doing your job to make money for racing can get very old, very fast. If you could spend eight hours each day on your riding skills rather than working on your bike or at the job, you would see some dramatic improvements.

One of the original ideas of sponsorship was to let skilled artists and craftsmen have the time to create their work. Use your sponsorship to create yourself as a better rider.

Treat sponsors in a business-like and friendly manner. Increased sales is their bottom line. Keep the business separate from your riding, but don't forget that it is part of the three main factors for success. They are: Good riding, good equipment and good sponsors.

Factory Rides

Sponsorship also brings about the possibility of a factory ride. The factories, and the people they listen to, are very good at spotting who has the potential to be a top-notch rider.

A word of caution: even though it has become ever more popular to take drugs in this society, this is something that smart team managers are on the lookout for. Riders who have a reputation for partying are not being looked on with favor. Drugs are like a decreasing-radius turn –they fool you into going in too fast, then make it very hard for you to get out.

In closing on the subject of sponsorship, a written agreement is <u>always</u> in order. If you obtain sponsorship, get the terms <u>in writing</u>–at least until you see how each other operates. Sometimes it's better to pay for supplies than to get them with invisible strings attached. Herein lies a great truth: **It often costs more to get things free than it does to pay for them.** Keep up your agreed-upon exchange with your sponsor and it should work out fine.

Taking drugs and racing is crazy. I don't want to ride with those guys and usually I don't have to.

From your sponsor you get money and stickers, etc. Money is payment for how well you expose the stickers and his name. Magazine photos really pump-up sponsors.

A Parting Word

Many things have not been included in this book because they do not have to do with the actual riding of a motorcycle. Track safety information, machine preparation and other valuable data are not in my area. Much of this has already been covered in the publication "How to Fly" by Joe Ziegler, who runs the Penguin Racing School at Loudon, New Hampshire and Bridgehampton, New York.

By the same token, all there is to say about riding is not in these pages. The material that is included is workable and will improve your riding if it's applied. It is meant to be applied and to be used.

Spend your $10 wisely, and most of all, have fun riding!

Appendix

Rider Checklist

1. **Oil at Proper Level**
   A. Engine
   B. Transmission
   C. Chain
   D. Forks

2. **Wheels Are In Line**

3. **Forks Don't Bind**

4. **Chain Adjusted**

5. **Tire Pressures Are Correct**
   A. Cold Pressures Front _____ Rear _____
   B. Hot Pressures Front _____ Rear _____

6. **Steering Head Bearings Tight**

7. **Front Axle Cap Bolts Tight**

8. **Axles Tight**

9. **Wheels Are Balanced**

10. **Controls Are Comfortable and Usable**

11. **Fork Travel Correct**
    (Forks should not bottom out or top out)

12. **Shock Travel Correct**
    (Shocks should not bottom out excessively but should use most of the shock travel.)

13. **Throttle Operates Smoothly**
    (Doesn't stick, no excessive free play.)

14. **Brakes Work Well**
    A. Pads are making good contact on disc.
    B. Pads are not binding disc.
    C. Enough pad material.

15. **Tires Have Enough Rubber**
    A. Unevenly worn or stepped tires can cause handling difficulties.
    B. Old racing tires dry out and become "greasy."
    C. Race tires work best when they have just been scrubbed in and have plenty of rubber.

16. **Enough Fuel**

17. **Master Link in Place**
    (Master link should be safety wired unless it is an endless chain.)

18. **Someone to Record Lap Times**

    Most of these items are not things that a technical inspector looks at. They are items that directly affect your ability to put your equipment to use as a racer. They ensure that you can make it around the track without major mishaps (enough fuel, etc.).

Race Day Record ①

Date _____

Track _____

Racing Organization _____

Length of Track _____

Number of Turns _____

Weather Conditions _____

Ambient Temperature _____

Elevation _____

Classes to be Run _____

Tires Run: Brand _____

Compound/Number _____ Front _____ Rear _____

Tire Pressure: Front—Cold _____ Rear—Cold _____

Front—Hot _____ Rear—Hot _____

Tire Mileage: Front _____ Rear _____

Jetting
Mains _____ Pilot _____ Air Correction _____ Air Screws _____

Needle _____ Slide _____ Float Level _____ Other _____

Gasoline Type _____

Gas/Oil Ratio _____

Ignition Timing _____

Spark Plug Heat Range _____

Cam Timing: Intake _____ Exhaust _____

Valve Adjustment: Intake _____ Exhaust _____

Gearing
Countershaft _____ Rear Sprocket _____ Overall Ratio _____

Shock Dampening
Front—Compression-Rebound _____ Rear—Compression-Rebound _____

Spring Settings
Front— Pre-Load _____ Rear—Pre-Load _____

Lap Times
Practice _____ Races _____

Position Each Lap _____

Points Earned _____

Prize Money Won _____

Comments _____

_____

_____

_____

Rider Checklist

1. **Oil at Proper Level**
   A. Engine
   B. Transmission
   C. Chain
   D. Forks

2. **Wheels Are In Line**

3. **Forks Don't Bind**

4. **Chain Adjusted**

5. **Tire Pressures Are Correct**
   A. Cold Pressures Front _____ Rear _____
   B. Hot Pressures Front _____ Rear _____

6. **Steering Head Bearings Tight**

7. **Front Axle Cap Bolts Tight**

8. **Axles Tight**

9. **Wheels Are Balanced**

10. **Controls Are Comfortable and Usable**

11. **Fork Travel Correct**
    (Forks should not bottom out or top out)

12. **Shock Travel Correct**
    (Shocks should not bottom out excessively but should use most of the shock travel.)

13. **Throttle Operates Smoothly**
    (Doesn't stick, no excessive free play.)

14. **Brakes Work Well**
    A. Pads are making good contact on disc.
    B. Pads are not binding disc.
    C. Enough pad material.

15. **Tires Have Enough Rubber**
    A. Unevenly worn or stepped tires can cause handling difficulties.
    B. Old racing tires dry out and become "greasy."
    C. Race tires work best when they have just been scrubbed in and have plenty of rubber.

16. **Enough Fuel**

17. **Master Link in Place**
    (Master link should be safety wired unless it is an endless chain.)

18. **Someone to Record Lap Times**

    Most of these items are not things that a technical inspector looks at. They are items that directly affect your ability to put your equipment to use as a racer. They ensure that you can make it around the track without major mishaps (enough fuel, etc.).

Race Day Record ②

Date _____

Track _____

Racing Organization _____

Length of Track _____

Number of Turns _____

Weather Conditions _____

Ambient Temperature _____

Elevation _____

Classes to be Run _____

Tires Run: Brand _____

Compound/Number _____ Front _____ Rear _____

Tire Pressure: Front—Cold _____ Rear—Cold _____

Front—Hot _____ Rear—Hot _____

Tire Mileage: Front _____ Rear _____

Jetting
Mains _____ Pilot _____ Air Correction _____ Air Screws _____

Needle _____ Slide _____ Float Level _____ Other _____

Gasoline Type _____

Gas/Oil Ratio _____

Ignition Timing _____

Spark Plug Heat Range _____

Cam Timing: Intake _____ Exhaust _____

Valve Adjustment: Intake _____ Exhaust _____

Gearing
Countershaft _____ Rear Sprocket _____ Overall Ratio _____

Shock Dampening
Front—Compression-Rebound _____ Rear—Compression-Rebound _____

Spring Settings
Front— Pre-Load _____ Rear—Pre-Load_____

Lap Times
Practice _____ Races _____

Position Each Lap _____

Points Earned _____

Prize Money Won _____

Comments _____

_____

_____

_____

_____

Rider Checklist

1. **Oil at Proper Level**
   A. Engine
   B. Transmission
   C. Chain
   D. Forks

2. **Wheels Are In Line**

3. **Forks Don't Bind**

4. **Chain Adjusted**

5. **Tire Pressures Are Correct**
   A. Cold Pressures Front _____ Rear _____
   B. Hot Pressures Front _____ Rear _____

6. **Steering Head Bearings Tight**

7. **Front Axle Cap Bolts Tight**

8. **Axles Tight**

9. **Wheels Are Balanced**

10. **Controls Are Comfortable and Usable**

11. **Fork Travel Correct**
    (Forks should not bottom out or top out)

12. **Shock Travel Correct**
    (Shocks should not bottom out excessively but should use most of the shock travel.)

13. **Throttle Operates Smoothly**
    (Doesn't stick, no excessive free play.)

14. **Brakes Work Well**
    A. Pads are making good contact on disc.
    B. Pads are not binding disc.
    C. Enough pad material.

15. **Tires Have Enough Rubber**
    A. Unevenly worn or stepped tires can cause handling difficulties.
    B. Old racing tires dry out and become "greasy."
    C. Race tires work best when they have just been scrubbed in and have plenty of rubber.

16. **Enough Fuel**

17. **Master Link in Place**
    (Master link should be safety wired unless it is an endless chain.)

18. **Someone to Record Lap Times**

    Most of these items are not things that a technical inspector looks at. They are items that directly affect your ability to put your equipment to use as a racer. They ensure that you can make it around the track without major mishaps (enough fuel, etc.).

Race Day Record ③

Date _____

Track _____

Racing Organization _____

Length of Track _____

Number of Turns _____

Weather Conditions _____

Ambient Temperature _____

Elevation _____

Classes to be Run _____

Tires Run: Brand _____

Compound/Number _____ Front _____ Rear _____

Tire Pressure: Front—Cold _____ Rear—Cold _____

Front—Hot _____ Rear—Hot _____

Tire Mileage: Front _____ Rear _____

Jetting
Mains _____ Pilot _____ Air Correction _____ Air Screws _____

Needle _____ Slide _____ Float Level _____ Other _____

Gasoline Type _____

Gas/Oil Ratio _____

Ignition Timing _____

Spark Plug Heat Range _____

Cam Timing: Intake _____ Exhaust _____

Valve Adjustment: Intake _____ Exhaust _____

Gearing
Countershaft _____ Rear Sprocket _____ Overall Ratio _____

Shock Dampening
Front—Compression-Rebound _____ Rear—Compression-Rebound _____

Spring Settings
Front— Pre-Load _____ Rear—Pre-Load_____

Lap Times
Practice _____ Races _____

Position Each Lap _____

Points Earned _____

Prize Money Won _____

Comments _____

_____

_____

_____

_____

Rider Checklist

1. **Oil at Proper Level**
   A. Engine
   B. Transmission
   C. Chain
   D. Forks

2. **Wheels Are In Line**

3. **Forks Don't Bind**

4. **Chain Adjusted**

5. **Tire Pressures Are Correct**
   A. Cold Pressures Front _____ Rear _____
   B. Hot Pressures Front _____ Rear _____

6. **Steering Head Bearings Tight**

7. **Front Axle Cap Bolts Tight**

8. **Axles Tight**

9. **Wheels Are Balanced**

10. **Controls Are Comfortable and Usable**

11. **Fork Travel Correct**
    (Forks should not bottom out or top out)

12. **Shock Travel Correct**
    (Shocks should not bottom out excessively but should use most of the shock travel.)

13. **Throttle Operates Smoothly**
    (Doesn't stick, no excessive free play.)

14. **Brakes Work Well**
    A. Pads are making good contact on disc.
    B. Pads are not binding disc.
    C. Enough pad material.

15. **Tires Have Enough Rubber**
    A. Unevenly worn or stepped tires can cause handling difficulties.
    B. Old racing tires dry out and become "greasy."
    C. Race tires work best when they have just been scrubbed in and have plenty of rubber.

16. **Enough Fuel**

17. **Master Link in Place**
    (Master link should be safety wired unless it is an endless chain.)

18. **Someone to Record Lap Times**

    Most of these items are not things that a technical inspector looks at. They are items that directly affect your ability to put your equipment to use as a racer. They ensure that you can make it around the track without major mishaps (enough fuel, etc.).

Race Day Record ④

Date _____

Track _____

Racing Organization _____

Length of Track _____

Number of Turns _____

Weather Conditions _____

Ambient Temperature _____

Elevation _____

Classes to be Run _____

Tires Run: Brand _____

Compound/Number _____ Front _____ Rear _____

Tire Pressure: Front—Cold _____ Rear—Cold _____

Front—Hot _____ Rear—Hot _____

Tire Mileage: Front _____ Rear _____

Jetting
Mains _____ Pilot _____ Air Correction _____ Air Screws _____

Needle _____ Slide _____ Float Level _____ Other _____

Gasoline Type _____

Gas/Oil Ratio _____

Ignition Timing _____

Spark Plug Heat Range _____

Cam Timing: Intake _____ Exhaust _____

Valve Adjustment: Intake _____ Exhaust _____

Gearing
Countershaft _____ Rear Sprocket _____ Overall Ratio _____

Shock Dampening
Front—Compression-Rebound _____ Rear—Compression-Rebound _____

Spring Settings
Front— Pre-Load _____ Rear—Pre-Load_____

Lap Times
Practice _____ Races _____

Position Each Lap _____

Points Earned _____

Prize Money Won _____

Comments _____

_____

_____

_____

_____

Rider Checklist

1. **Oil at Proper Level**
   A. Engine
   B. Transmission
   C. Chain
   D. Forks

2. **Wheels Are In Line**

3. **Forks Don't Bind**

4. **Chain Adjusted**

5. **Tire Pressures Are Correct**
   A. Cold Pressures Front _____ Rear _____
   B. Hot Pressures Front _____ Rear _____

6. **Steering Head Bearings Tight**

7. **Front Axle Cap Bolts Tight**

8. **Axles Tight**

9. **Wheels Are Balanced**

10. **Controls Are Comfortable and Usable**

11. **Fork Travel Correct**
    (Forks should not bottom out or top out)

12. **Shock Travel Correct**
    (Shocks should not bottom out excessively but should use most of the shock travel.)

13. **Throttle Operates Smoothly**
    (Doesn't stick, no excessive free play.)

14. **Brakes Work Well**
    A. Pads are making good contact on disc.
    B. Pads are not binding disc.
    C. Enough pad material.

15. **Tires Have Enough Rubber**
    A. Unevenly worn or stepped tires can cause handling difficulties.
    B. Old racing tires dry out and become "greasy."
    C. Race tires work best when they have just been scrubbed in and have plenty of rubber.

16. **Enough Fuel**

17. **Master Link in Place**
    (Master link should be safety wired unless it is an endless chain.)

18. **Someone to Record Lap Times**

Most of these items are not things that a technical inspector looks at. They are items that directly affect your ability to put your equipment to use as a racer. They ensure that you can make it around the track without major mishaps (enough fuel, etc.).

Race Day Record ⑤

Date _____

Track _____

Racing Organization _____

Length of Track _____

Number of Turns _____

Weather Conditions _____

Ambient Temperature _____

Elevation _____

Classes to be Run _____

Tires Run: Brand _____

Compound/Number _____ Front _____ Rear _____

Tire Pressure: Front—Cold _____ Rear—Cold _____

Front—Hot _____ Rear—Hot _____

Tire Mileage: Front _____ Rear _____

Jetting
Mains _____ Pilot _____ Air Correction _____ Air Screws _____

Needle _____ Slide _____ Float Level _____ Other _____

Gasoline Type _____

Gas/Oil Ratio _____

Ignition Timing _____

Spark Plug Heat Range _____

Cam Timing: Intake _____ Exhaust _____

Valve Adjustment: Intake _____ Exhaust _____

Gearing
Countershaft _____ Rear Sprocket _____ Overall Ratio _____

Shock Dampening
Front—Compression-Rebound _____ Rear—Compression-Rebound _____

Spring Settings
Front— Pre-Load _____ Rear—Pre-Load _____

Lap Times
Practice _____ Races _____

Position Each Lap _____

Points Earned _____

Prize Money Won _____

Comments _____

_____

_____

_____

_____

Notes

THE HOW-TO TRIO

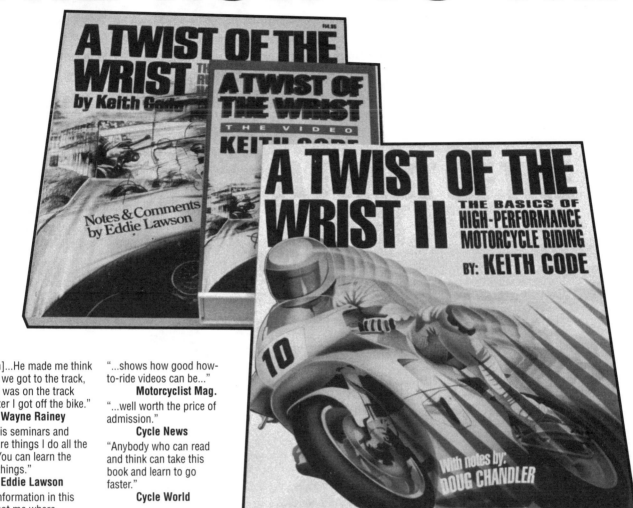

"[Keith]...He made me think before we got to the track, while I was on the track and after I got off the bike."
Wayne Rainey

"...in his seminars and book are things I do all the time. You can learn the same things."
Eddie Lawson

"The information in this book got me where I am now in roadracing."
Doug Chandler

"...shows how good how-to-ride videos can be..."
Motorcyclist Mag.

"...well worth the price of admission."
Cycle News

"Anybody who can read and think can take this book and learn to go faster."
Cycle World

You've got to ask yourself, "If I don't have them, HOW MUCH DON'T I KNOW?" It's a fair question. You already know what you do know, let's not argue about that. But, with nearly 300 pages of written material, photos, illustrations and diagrams plus over 1-3/4 hours of action video on riding...you've got to wonder.

Here are simple, plain language, straight facts about riding, not complicated science: they're written for you. They are definitely not read or view-once-and-shelve-it items. In fact, the average reader cracked "A Twist Of The Wrist, Volume I" over 10 times and watched the video 8. Find out what hundreds of thousands of riders and racers DO KNOW.

A TWIST OF THE WRIST - ORDER FORM

☐ **A TWIST OF THE WRIST, VOLUME I** — $14.95 + S&H $2.05 — California residents add $1.23
☐ **A TWIST OF THE WRIST, VOLUME II** — $17.95 + S&H $3.00 — California residents add $1.50
☐ **A TWIST OF THE WRIST, VIDEO** — $39.95 + S&H $2.95 — California residents add $3.30
☐ **THE SOFT SCIENCE OF ROADRACING MOTORCYCLES, book** — $14.95 + S&H $2.05 — California residents add $1.23

Name _____

Address _____

City _____ State _____ Zip _____

Telephones (Home/Work) _____

Signature _____

Credit Card No._____ Exp. Date _____

Total _____

VISA   MC   DISCOVER   CHECK

Mail to:
CALIFORNIA SUPERBIKE SCHOOL
PO Box 3107
Hollywood, CA 90078

ORDER BY PHONE - CALL:
Phone 1-800-530-3350
FAX 213 484-9184

RAINEY'S WAY

After 20 years of racing **WAYNE RAINEY** is at the top. Starting his roadracing career with **KEITH CODE** as his trainer brought both of them to a new understanding of how a racer thinks. That thinking is written down in **"THE SOFT SCIENCE OF ROADRACING MOTORCYCLES."** Wayne says, *"You really can change your ideas and go faster.* Each chapter has questions and drills that will improve your racing. *"I think the guys coming up need to do these steps."* Buy and read **"THE SOFT SCIENCE OF ROADRACING MOTORCYCLES"** today! 120 photos, diagrams and illustrations, 166 pages.

. . . .

"THE SOFT SCIENCE OF ROADRACING MOTORCYCLES"